A Clinician's Guide to Opioids

• HAZELDEN CLINICAL PRACTICE SERIES •

A Clinician's Guide to Opioids

From the experts at the Hazelden Betty Ford Foundation

Hazelden
Publishing

Hazelden Publishing
Center City, Minnesota 55012
hazelden.org/bookstore

ISBN: 978-1-61649-784-2

Editor's notes

This publication is not intended as a substitute for the advice of health care professionals.

Readers should be aware that websites listed in this work may have changed or disappeared between when this work was written and when it is read.

Alcoholics Anonymous, AA, and the Big Book are registered trademarks of Alcoholics Anonymous World Services, Inc.

The case studies in this guide are from actual clinical encounters with a patient or a composite representing the experience of one or more patients. The names have been changed for privacy.

The name "COR-12™" is a trademark and may not be used in any way without the written permission of Hazelden Publishing as the publisher. Use of this name in a treatment setting as part of implementation of the COR-12 program and the purchase of materials from Hazelden Publishing is allowed.

Cover design: Kathi Dunn, Dunn + Associates
Typesetting: Jessica Ess, Hillspring Books

CONTENTS

ACKNOWLEDGMENTS

The following people shared their clinical and medical expertise in the hopes that this guide will help educate and inform health practitioners who serve patients seeking recovery from opioid use disorder.

Jordan Hansen is the Comprehensive Opioid Response with the Twelve Steps (COR-12) program manager at Hazelden Publishing. Hansen is an experienced clinician, consultant, writer, and speaker focused on assisting communities and organizations adopting evidence-based practices for the treatment of substance use disorders. He manages Hazelden Publishing's Clinical Systems training and consultation programs, including helping implement effective medication-assisted programming for the treatment of opioid use disorder. Hansen's experience as a clinician within residential, long-term, and outpatient levels of care informs all his work, aiming to combine cutting-edge, evidence-based treatment approaches with the wisdom found in peer-supported recovery.

Cathy Stone is the COR-12 program manager at the Hazelden Betty Ford Foundation in St. Paul. Stone joined the Hazelden Betty Ford Foundation as a counselor in residential treatment before becoming manager of outpatient treatment. Stone has expertise in opioid addiction treatment, trauma-informed treatment, and treatment of female populations. She holds a bachelor of arts degree in women's studies from Colorado College and a master of arts in public affairs from the University of Minnesota. She received her master of arts in addiction counseling from the Hazelden Betty Ford Graduate School of Addiction Studies.

The following people also provided their expertise in the development and evolution of the COR-12 program; this expertise included valuable real-world practice to help inform this guide. Learn more about COR-12 in the "About the Hazelden Betty Ford Foundation and COR-12" section on page viii.

Marvin D. Seppala, MD, chief medical officer at the Hazelden Betty Ford Foundation, is a national expert on addiction treatment, pharmacological treatments, and integration of evidence-based practices. Seppala served as a board member of the American Society of Addiction Medicine (ASAM) for several years and is a national expert on addiction treatment. Seppala is author of *Clinician's Guide to the Twelve Step Principles* (McGraw-Hill/Hazelden, 2002). He coauthored *When Painkillers Become Dangerous* (Hazelden Publishing, 2004), followed by *Pain-Free Living for Drug-Free People* (Hazelden Publishing, 2005). He is also the author of *Prescription Painkillers: History, Pharmacology, and Treatment* (Hazelden Publishing, 2010). He has appeared as a guest on CBS's *The Early Show*, CNN, and

National Public Radio. He has been quoted in the *New York Times,* the *Washington Post, USA Today, Newsweek,* and the *Wall Street Journal.*

Bruce Larson, MA, LADC, CADC, has worked in the field of addiction counseling for more than thirty-eight years. He is a clinical consultant for the Hazelden Betty Ford Foundation and was previously a clinical director at the Hazelden Betty Ford Foundation's Center City campus, starting in 2001. Larson also served as a clinical supervisor and director of Hazelden's counselor training program. Larson is a former member of the Hazelden Betty Ford Foundation's Senior Leadership Council and has taught for the counselor training program and the Hazelden Betty Ford Graduate School of Addiction Studies for twenty-five years. Larson earned a master of arts degree from St. Mary's University of Minnesota and holds active addiction counselor licenses in both Minnesota and Wisconsin. Larson has been a national voice for addiction treatment, having served as board member and chair of the education committee for the Institute for Chemical Dependency Professionals, as board member and chair of the National Standards for the International Certification Reciprocity Consortium, and as a conference-planning committee member for the Minnesota Association of Resources for Recovery and Chemical Health. Larson is the author of *A Design for Living* for DUI/DWI offenders (Hazelden Publishing, 1994) and *The Disease of Addiction: Symptoms and Phases* workbook (Hazelden Publishing, 1999).

About the Hazelden Betty Ford Foundation and COR-12

The Hazelden Betty Ford Foundation is a force of healing and hope for individuals, families, and communities affected by addiction to alcohol and other drugs. It is the nation's largest nonprofit treatment provider, with a legacy that began in 1949 and includes the 1982 founding of the Betty Ford Center.

With seventeen sites in California, Minnesota, Oregon, Illinois, New York, Florida, Massachusetts, Colorado, and Texas, the Foundation offers prevention and recovery solutions nationwide and across the entire continuum of care for youth and adults. It includes the largest recovery publishing house in the country, a fully accredited graduate school of addiction studies, an addiction research center, an education arm for medical professionals, and a unique children's program and is the nation's leader in advocacy and policy for treatment and recovery.

Addiction treatment at the Hazelden Betty Ford Foundation integrates the cornerstone Twelve Step practices of mutual support along with multidisciplinary clinical care, evidence-based therapies, and the latest research in brain science. This includes an initiative, started in 2012, to create and implement a new opioid addiction treatment program to address the opioid epidemic in our nation and to improve treatment outcomes for opioid use disorder, which have historically been poor. The resulting Hazelden Betty Ford Foundation program, Comprehensive Opioid Response with the Twelve Steps (COR-12), is an evidence-based, medication-assisted treatment program that can be implemented in a variety of health care settings. The program integrates the use of medication-assisted treatment (such as use of naltrexone or buprenorphine/naloxone) with psychotherapies, opioid-specific group therapy and patient education, and a strong Twelve Step orientation to improve psychosocial functioning, enrich relationships, and foster a healthier lifestyle—all keys to a lasting recovery. (See chapter 8 for more about the COR-12 program.)

In 2018, the Butler Center for Research analyzed and published data from the Hazelden Betty Ford Foundation's first study of adult opioid use disorder patients who attended residential treatment and participated in the COR-12 program. This study analyzed the progress of 259 patients in the COR-12 program. The majority of these patients had multiple substance use disorders (in addition to opioid use disorder); they had multiple co-occurring mental health disorders and had attended multiple treatment episodes for substance use disorders prior to entering the COR-12 program at the Hazelden Betty Ford Foundation.

This study of the COR-12 program revealed high abstinence rates from alcohol and other drugs. Continuous abstinence rates overall were very high, particularly when considering the clinical severity of these patients. Approximately 90 percent of buprenorphine- and naltrexone-compliant patients retained abstinence one month after treatment, and 82 percent of naltrexone-compliant patients retained abstinence six months after treatment.[1] Even the patients who were not on any medication-assisted treatment did very well, with 74 percent of the non-medication pathway COR-12 patients retaining abstinence six months after treatment. Treatment retention was also high, with 92 percent of COR-12 patients successfully completing treatment. (Note that medication use did not result in higher treatment-completion rates.) These results suggest that the COR-12 program holds a great deal of promise in helping individuals with opioid use disorder achieve recovery.

PREFACE

This guide includes current research and education on opioid misuse and effective prevention, screening, assessment, and treatment, including the use of medication-assisted treatment options for opioid use disorder. This guide includes clinical best practices in treatment and detailed case studies that illustrate common clinical challenges faced by providers in addiction treatment settings and suggested solutions.

The intended audience for this guide includes drug and alcohol counselors, psychotherapists, physicians, drug court and other legal professionals, and anyone who wants to better understand the effects and treatment of opioid use disorders. This guide is a clinical tool and is not intended to be a substitute for clinical judgment; neither is the information contained here intended to direct treatment professionals to provide treatment outside of their scope of practice.

Definitions

Throughout this guide, the terms *opioid use disorder* and *opioid addiction* are used interchangeably. The choice of terms used is often only stylistic. While the treatment of opioid use disorders is the main focus of this book, there are some general principles that apply to the treatment of all substance use disorders.

In this guide the generic terms for medications are used rather than specific brand names. There is ongoing advancement in medications used as an adjunct to treatment for opioid use disorders. Formulations and associated brand names are quickly changing as new brands attempt to better address medication-adherence challenges and better target medicines to the underlying mechanisms of disease.

At the time of this printing, buprenorphine systemic medication includes brand names Butrans, Subutex, Belbuca, and Buprenex. Buprenorphine/naloxone systemic medication includes brand names Suboxone, Zubsolv, and Bunavail. Naltrexone systemic medication includes brand names Vivitrol, Revia, and Depade.

■ ■ ■

INTRODUCTION

For Whom Is This Guide Designed?

This guide and related resources are designed for use by any professional who works on the "front lines" with patients seeking help for opioid use disorders. This includes alcohol and drug counselors, administrators, physicians, nurses, mental health practitioners, case managers, social workers, and more. This guide covers best practices on the entire continuum of care in prevention, intervention, treatment, and continuing care planning with patients with opioid use disorders.

How to Use This Guide

In this guide, Part 1: Education provides in-depth information about opioids, including current research and statistics about opioid use, the problem of the opioid epidemic, demographics of opioid use, effects on the brain and body, special populations and opioid use, and an overview of treatment of opioid use disorders.

Part 2: Clinical Practice covers best practices in clinical evaluation and treatment in patients with an opioid use disorder. This includes screening and assessment, detoxification, withdrawal, evaluating medication pathways, and using medication-assisted treatment. It covers common clinical challenges in treatment such as patient engagement, patients leaving against medical advice, and transitioning patients between levels of care.

Part 3: Case Studies addresses real-world treatment challenges examined through detailed case studies. This content is based on the lived clinical expertise of counselors and other experts at the Hazelden Betty Ford Foundation.

Some of the information presented in this guide builds on the Comprehensive Opioid Response with the Twelve Steps (COR-12) treatment approach created and used by the Hazelden Betty Ford Foundation in response to the nation's epidemic of prescription painkiller addiction and rising death toll from accidental overdose of opioids. The COR-12 treatment approach includes enhanced treatment programming to include new tracks for those with opioid dependence. This innovative programming encompasses the whole spectrum of recovery—from pre-recovery to recovery initiation to ongoing and lifelong recovery support services. The COR-12 treatment path includes customized group therapy and lectures as well as use of extended, adjunctive medication-assisted treatment (MAT) as a means to assist people to a stable, Twelve Step–based recovery lifestyle and ultimate abstinence from opioids. The COR-12 program was created and is evolving with the support of a cross-disciplinary team of the Foundation's medical, clinical, research, administrative, and communications professionals to research, study, and implement solutions to the problem. The Hazelden Betty Ford Foundation believes the COR-12 approach offers patients the best chances of long-term recovery from opioid addiction. Much of the material in this guide is adapted or excerpted from the COR-12 Implementation Guide, *Integrating the Twelve Steps with Medication-Assisted Treatment for Opioid Use Disorder* by Marvin D. Seppala and Bruce Larson (Center City, MN: Hazelden Publishing, 2015). Additional excerpts are from *Heroin and Prescription Painkillers: A Toolkit for Community Action,* updated and expanded edition (Center City, MN: Hazelden Publishing, 2016).

Part 1 has four chapters. In Chapter 1: Understanding Opioids, there is information about different types of opioids and the scale of the opioid epidemic, as well as information about patients seeking treatment for opioid use disorder. Chapter 2: Effects of Opioids on the Brain and Body covers how opioid use impacts the user's brain and body and offers information about the dangerous consequences of opioid use. Chapter 3: Opioids in Special Populations explores opioid issues specific to adolescents and young adults, pregnant women, patients with medical comorbidities, and those with co-occurring mental health disorders. Chapter 4: Overview of Treatment and Recovery covers access to treatment, types of services, treatment in criminal justice populations, and a brief overview of evidence-based methods.

Part 2 of this guide has five chapters. In Chapter 5: Screening and Evaluation, there is information on diagnostic methods, screening in primary care settings, assessment, brief intervention, evaluating medication pathways, and referral to treatment. Chapter 6: Effective Treatment of Opioid Use Disorder covers the commonly used evidence-based practices in treating opioid use disorder. It also covers initiation of treatment and common challenges and concerns in treatment. Chapter 7: Medications Used to Treat Opioid Use Disorder covers the medications naltrexone, buprenorphine, and methadone. Chapter 8: MAT as an Integrated Evidence-Based Practice offers research supporting the use of MAT, using MAT in conjunction with other evidence-based practices, engaging family members, MAT and Twelve Step groups, evaluating use of MAT for individual patients, and more. Chapter 9: Continuing Care Planning offers research supporting recovery management, guidance on transitioning patients into lower levels of care such as sober living or use of a recovery coach, and ultimately into self-management using community or peer support.

Part 3 of this guide includes Chapter 10: Treatment Challenges and Solutions, where four case studies are offered as examples of how to put the information and best practices in this guide into action in clinical practice with patients. It covers four common challenges in the treatment of opioid use disorders and ways to successfully address these challenges.

The appendices at the back of the book provide useful resources, including Appendix A: Screening, Assessment, and Diagnostic Tools; Appendix B: Peer Support Resources; and Appendix C: Suggested Education Resources.

■ ■ ■

Part 1

Education

1

Understanding Opioids

This chapter provides an overview of the opioid epidemic, including basic information about what opioids are, the consequences of opioid use, the alarming statistics of opioid use and overdose, and a description of the kind of treatment needed to meet this serious epidemic.

What Are Opioids?

Opioids are a class of drugs that are derived from or simulate the effects of the pain-relieving compounds found in opium. Opium is the dried sap of the opium poppy plant (*papaver somniferum*). This plant grows throughout Asia, North Africa, South America, and the Middle East.

Opium has been used for thousands of years to relieve pain, calm anxiety, and help people sleep. But in more modern times we've begun to refine and extract other drugs from it. Morphine was the first drug refined from opium. Others quickly followed, including heroin and codeine. All of these are created directly from compounds found in opium.

Some opioids are *semisynthetic* or *synthetic*. This means they're partially or completely manufactured using chemicals with properties that are similar to opium. Examples include many of the prescription pain medications available today, such as the very potent synthetic opioids fentanyl and carfentanil, which are sometimes used medically in anesthesia.

Recently, there has been an increase in the illegal manufacturing and distribution of illicit versions of extremely potent opioids such as fentanyl, which is fifty times more potent than heroin.[1] Among the more than 64,000 drug overdose deaths estimated in 2016, the sharpest increase was in deaths specifically related to fentanyl and fentanyl analogs (synthetic opioids) found in more than 20,000 of those overdose deaths.[2] More information is located in this guide under the section on synthetic opioids.

Opioid versus *Opiate*

A note about terminology: *Opioid* is an umbrella term that refers to all the natural, semisynthetic, and synthetic painkillers derived from the opium poppy. The more commonly used term *opiate* applies only to products created directly from the opium poppy.

The most commonly used opioids include heroin and the following prescription or over-the-counter drugs:

- morphine (Kadian, Avinza)
- codeine
- methadone (Dolophine)
- hydromorphone (Dilaudid)
- hydrocodone (Vicodin)
- oxycodone (Percocet, OxyContin)
- fentanyl (Sublimaze, Actiq)
- meperidine (Demerol)

Heroin can be a white, gray, brown, or black powder or a black tarlike substance. It is taken orally, smoked, snorted, used as a suppository, or injected into a muscle or vein. Heroin often goes by the street names *smack, H, ska, tar, dope, china white, holly, horse,* and *junk.*

On the street, prescription opioids also go by many names, including *oxy, OC, M, sister morphine, hydros, tabs,* and *demmies.*

Prescription opioids come in a variety of forms:

- a time-release capsule or tablet
- a liquid, such as cough syrups containing codeine
- syringes containing injectable substances
- suppositories
- patches that adhere to the skin
- lozenges that dissolve in the mouth

The Opioid Epidemic

As opioid use disorder and its accompanying problems of overdose and death have reached epidemic levels across the United States, it is perhaps not surprising to learn the issue reaches across all divisions of race, economic status, and gender. Many factors are involved in the current opioid epidemic. One is our country's insatiable demand for opioids. While Americans make up only 4.6 percent of the world's population, they consume 80 percent of the global opioid supply. This is driven in part by the number of Americans who live with chronic pain—about a hundred million. This is more than those with cancer, heart disease, and diabetes combined.[3]

Of the 20.5 million Americans age twelve or older who had a substance use disorder in 2015, approximately two million had a substance use disorder involving prescription pain relievers, and 591,000 had a substance use disorder involving heroin.[4] Drug overdose is the leading cause of accidental death in the United States, with 52,404 lethal drug overdoses in 2015.[5] Opioid addiction is driving this epidemic, with 20,101 overdose deaths related to prescription pain relievers and 12,990 overdose deaths related to heroin in 2015.[6]

From 1999 to 2016, more than 630,000 people died from drug overdoses in the United States.[7] According to the U.S. Centers for Disease Control and Prevention (CDC), approximately 115 Americans die each day from an opioid overdose.[8]

Economic Impact

Communities affected by opioid addiction pay a high price in terms of legal expenses, law enforcement, workplace costs, hospitalizations, and deaths. Whether directly affected by addiction in the family or in the form of higher taxes and medical costs, everyone is touched by it. According to an estimate from the CDC, the total economic burden of prescription opioid misuse alone in the United States is $78.5 billion a year. This figure includes the costs related to health care, lost productivity, addiction treatment, and criminal justice involvement.[9]

A more detailed look at the $78.5 billion a year reveals these cost breakdowns:

- $28 billion was in health care and treatment costs.
- $20 billion was in lost productivity.
- $21 billion was in costs related to cases of fatal overdose, including lost productivity and health care.
- $7.7 billion was in criminal justice–related costs.[10]

The economic and personal costs of opioid use are substantial, particularly when health care costs for people who abuse opioids are compared to costs for those who do not. One study revealed that health care costs for opioid abusers were eight times higher ($15,884 compared to $1,830) than for nonabusers.[11]

Drug diversion puts a tremendous strain on the health care system. The financial incentive for theft is high. Prescription painkillers are often sold on the black market at markups of more than 700 percent over their retail price. Theft or diversion of a controlled substance is a felony, even for one pill. Criminal prosecutions and lawsuits rightfully follow, and those costs are ultimately paid by society through higher prices, taxes, extra security measures, hospital stays, emergency room care, insurance fraud, rehabilitation costs, and broken public trust. According to the Coalition Against Insurance Fraud, prescription drug diversion costs insurers more than $72 billion a year.[12] These costs represent only a partial measure of the problems related to drug diversion.

The cost society pays in disease, crime, and lost productivity from heroin use is widespread and deep. The CDC estimates that nearly one-quarter of all HIV/AIDS cases in the United States since the 1980s can be traced back to dirty needles used for illegal drugs. Approximately 2,224 HIV diagnoses in the United States in 2016 were attributed to injection drug use, and 1,201 were attributed to male-to-male sexual contact and injection drug use.[13] When heroin use swells in any geographic area, so does crime. Burglary rates rise, and more people turn to other sources of cash—including prostitution—to support their drug use. This translates into increased costs for law enforcement as well as social services. Moreover, people focused on attaining their next bag of heroin often neglect their own self-care and especially the care of their children.

Types of Opioids

The class of drugs called opioids includes the illegal drug heroin, synthetic opioids such as fentanyl, and pain relievers available legally by prescription, such as oxycodone, hydrocodone, codeine, morphine, and many others. The details for each drug and routes of administration are described below.

Prescription Painkillers

Prescription painkillers include drugs such as morphine, codeine, hydrocodone, oxycodone, fentanyl, and meperidine. These drugs are very effective for relieving acute pain. For people who are recovering from surgery or an accident, these drugs provide relief like no other remedy. They are the most powerful, useful medications for moderate to severe pain relief that are available.

Most people who follow their prescription and doctor's recommendations do not develop an opioid use disorder. However, even when the medications are used as prescribed, people can develop a tolerance to the drugs and experience withdrawal symptoms when they stop. Once addicted, people might seek alternate forms of opioid relief, such as other prescription drugs or heroin, on the street.

How many people are using opioids? Legitimate medical use must be separated from nonmedical misuse. Prescriptions for opioids have increased significantly.

According to the CDC, opioid prescribing continues to fuel the epidemic. In 2014, almost two million Americans abused or were dependent on prescription opioids.[14] Every day, more than one thousand people are treated in emergency departments for misusing prescription opioids.[15]

Prescription opioids act on the same brain systems as heroin and are dangerous when used for nonmedical purposes.

There is a perception among some individuals who use, abuse, or misuse prescription opioids that these drugs are safer than illicit street drugs because doctors prescribe them. In reality, nonmedical use of prescription and over-the-counter medications can be equally as addictive and dangerous. This is especially true when opioids are taken with alcohol or other drugs, including other prescription drugs, which increases the risk of adverse health effects, including overdose.

The large number of opioid prescriptions is of special concern because the vast majority of the drugs involved in overdose deaths come from drug diversion, meaning they were taken by someone other than the person on the prescription. More than three out of four people who misuse prescription painkillers obtain drugs prescribed for someone else.[16] People who engaged in nonmedical use of prescription opioids were nineteen times more likely to use heroin for the first time than people who had not.[17]

Most prescription drugs are dispensed orally in tablets, but individuals who misuse these drugs sometimes crush the tablets and snort the powder or dissolve it in a liquid and inject it. This hastens the entry of the drug into the bloodstream and the brain and amplifies its effects.[18] Additionally, some tablets are specially designed to release a certain amount of medicine over time. Seeking to get high, an individual may crush these time-release tablets to snort or dissolve and inject the medicine. In this manner, a dose intended to work over a twelve-hour period of time hits the central nervous system all at once, amplifying its effects and greatly increasing the risk of overdose.[19]

A study published in 2010 found that routes of administration in nonmedical use of prescription opioids varied sharply between urban and rural users. Urban users were far more likely to swallow the pills, while snorting and injection were more common among rural users. Among the rural users participating in the study, hydrocodone, methadone, and oxycodone were more frequently snorted, while injection was most common for hydromorphone and morphine. Rural study participants also reported high rates of intravenous injection of certain drugs, with 67 percent of hydromorphone users and 63 percent of morphine users having injected the drugs.[20]

Synthetic Opioids

Synthetic opioids are a category of psychoactive substances that are not naturally occurring and that are either known to be opiates or have opiate-like effects. Synthetic opioids, such as fentanyl and carfentanil, are sometimes used medically in

Duplicating this page is illegal. Do not duplicate without the publisher's written permission.

7

anesthesia. Fentanyl was discovered in the 1960s for use in surgery and expanded in the 1990s as a prescription medication for pain.

The synthetic opioid carfentanil is a powerful derivative of fentanyl. According to the Drug Enforcement Administration (DEA), carfentanil is a synthetic opioid that is ten thousand times more potent than morphine and one hundred times more potent than fentanyl, which itself is fifty times more potent than heroin.[21] Powerful synthetic opioids such as fentanyl and carfentanil produce the same effect on the reward system of the body and the brain as other types of opioids do. However, they are far more potent, and their effects are increased when they are injected. This higher potency and rapid onset from injection increases the risk for dependence, as well as increases the likelihood of overdose and death.[22]

Fentanyl and fentanyl analogs, such as carfentanil, are also produced illicitly in the form of a very potent powder that can be snorted, injected, or pressed into pill form and taken orally. Recent years have seen a sharp increase in the manufacture of illicit versions of fentanyl, which, due to their dangerous potency, are responsible for nearly one-third of the 64,000 opioid-related overdose deaths reported in 2016.[23] According to a 2016 CDC report, there was an 80 percent increase in fatal overdoses involving fentanyl and other synthetic opioids in only one year (2013–2014).[24] While this sharp increase is largely attributed to illicitly manufactured synthetic opioids, it is also due to how powerful these synthetic opioids are in comparison to other prescription opioids.

Individuals who are misusing opioid painkillers may eventually seek more potent, easier-to-obtain, less expensive drugs—and they often find this in drugs such as fentanyl. Unlike heroin, fentanyl and its analogs are fairly easily and affordably created in a lab and then sold illicitly to offer users an affordable (less expensive per dose than heroin), yet deadly, high. Much of the illicit fentanyl found in the United States is manufactured in China, Mexico, and Canada, and the number of law enforcement seizures involving fentanyl increased from less than 1,000 to a whopping 13,000 in the two-year span between 2013 and 2015.[25] Users may also encounter illicit opioids through counterfeit pills intentionally designed to look like commonly known versions of prescription opioids (such as hydrocodone) or benzodiazepines.[26]

As with other types of drugs, the illicitly manufactured versions of synthetic opioids are the most dangerous, as users have no way of knowing how potent the drugs are or exactly what they contain. In some cases, synthetic opioids are added to other illicit drugs, including heroin, producing an especially high risk for overdose and death.[27]

Heroin

Heroin is a highly addictive opioid that is illegal and has no accepted medical use in the United States. Heroin is found in two forms: either as a white or brownish powder or as a black substance that can be sticky like goo or hard like coal. This is sometimes called black tar heroin.[28] In its purest form, heroin is a white powder that is usually "cut" or diluted by adding sugars, starch, powdered milk, or quinine. Heroin in this pure form is often smoked or snorted, making it a popular method for new and first-time users, because it avoids the negative stigma of intravenous injection—or shooting up.[29] The dark color associated with black tar heroin is a result of impurities left behind from crude methods of processing. Heroin in this less pure form is usually dissolved, diluted, and injected into veins, into muscles, or under the skin.

Heroin use has increased in the United States, including among groups who historically had low rates of heroin use, such as women, individuals with private insurance, and those with higher incomes.[30] About 435,000 people age twelve or older were current heroin users in 2014, a slight increase from 2013. According to the CDC, from 2015 to 2016, heroin overdose death rates increased by 19.5 percent, with nearly 15,500 people dying in 2016. In 2016, males age twenty-five to forty-four had the highest heroin death rate at 15.5 per 100,000, which was an increase of 17.4 percent from 2015.[31]

Heroin is no longer a crisis of urban areas and inner cities alone. Suburban and rural areas of the country are reporting record levels of hospital admissions for overdoses and criminal activity associated with heroin trafficking.

Heroin is cheaper and easier to get on the street than prescription opioids. As a result, first-time use of heroin among people age twelve and older in the United States spiked from 90,000 in 2006 to 169,000 in 2013.[32] Heroin use has more than doubled in the past decade among young adults age eighteen to twenty-five.[33]

The pathway to heroin use now commonly starts with misuse of prescription medications, then moves to heroin as a cheaper alternative. Past misuse of prescription opioids is the strongest risk factor for heroin initiation and use, specifically among persons who report past-year dependence or abuse. The increased availability of heroin, combined with its relatively low price (compared with diverted prescription opioids) and high purity appear to be major drivers of the upward trend in heroin use and overdose. It's estimated that 80 percent of heroin users start by misusing prescription opioids,[34] and a 2014 survey of people in treatment for opioid addiction found that 94 percent reported they chose to use heroin because prescription opioids were "far more expensive and harder to obtain."[35]

Heroin use carries the same risk of overdose as prescription opioids, with the added danger of lack of control over the purity of the drug, along with the risk of it being contaminated with other drugs (including potent synthetic opioids such as fentanyl and fentanyl analogues such as carfentanil).[36] Because heroin is typically injected, it also places users at increased risk of bloodborne diseases such as HIV and hepatitis, sexually transmitted infections (STIs), and other health concerns.[37]

Demographics of Patients Seeking Treatment

For individuals seeking treatment for opioid use disorder, the Hazelden Betty Ford Foundation has noted three main demographics.

- Patient 1 is dependent on prescription painkillers. These are people who do not meet criteria for a substance use disorder but feel "psychologically dependent" on opioids. They want to stop their pain medication, but they just don't know how to cope with the physical misery that inevitably entails.
- Patient 2 is a young heroin addict, age seventeen to thirty.
- Patient 3 is addicted to prescription painkillers, age twenty to fifty.

How Patients Differ

Patients fitting patient profile 1 are physically dependent on opioids, and they experience all the issues related to that. But when they are stabilized, their behaviors are actually exceptionally easy to control. They can benefit from recovery tools applied to their co-occurring pain diagnosis, and they can eventually manage their medication very easily. It is easy to focus on medication-based interventions for this patient population.

Patient profile 2, people addicted to heroin, comprises a population of patients who are more deeply attached to the drug at a younger age. In people using heroin, the chemical brain lesion is much more severe. This is the most difficult patient population to treat, but also very rewarding. These patients often arrive stuck in the precontemplation stage of change; they may have attended treatment several times but frequently relapsed back to drug use. These patients are at the greatest risk to relapse and die.

A large percentage of young heroin addicts come to the Hazelden Betty Ford Foundation program after attendance at several residential treatment programs. Often, the family no longer has the resources to send them to residential treatment. Many of these patients benefit from a medication such as naltrexone to help reduce their craving and relapse rumination. Using the medication allows these patients time to stabilize and engage in treatment.

With patient profile 3, people addicted to prescription painkillers, the scope of the problem is large. There are 13.5 million people in America who take opioid medications on a daily basis. The best estimates say that, at a minimum, 40 percent of them regularly misuse or abuse their medications: They take medications that aren't theirs. They have multiple doctors and are buying pills illicitly. They are often very functional in their addiction and will delay seeking treatment because they are unaware of treatment options, such as outpatient services, that could help them and fit within their schedule.

These patients often participate in outpatient programming at night so they can continue to hold down their day job. These patients often do very well in treatment as they often have more distress tolerance and social reinforcement to support the benefits of developing a successful recovery. Typically, these patients are older, more self-motivated, and more compliant. At the Hazelden Betty Ford Foundation, we see a very low relapse rate within this population.

▪ ▪ ▪

2

Effects of Opioids on the Brain and Body

Opioids are drugs that work by binding to the opioid receptors in the brain, spinal cord, and other areas of the body. All opioids, including heroin, prescription medications (such as painkillers like hydrocodone), and synthetic opioids (such as fentanyl and carfentanil), work through this same mechanism of action. Whether they are prescription medications or street drugs like heroin, the effects of opioids (and many other drugs) depend on how much a person takes and how the drug is administered. If the opioid is injected, it acts faster and more intensely. If opioids are swallowed as pills, they take longer to reach the brain.

Opioids and the Brain's Reward Center

Studies of long-term prescription opioid users who have developed opioid dependence have revealed structural and functional changes in their brains. These changes were found in areas of the brain associated with regulating impulse control, in addition to functions governing reward and motivational responses.[1] Researchers studying the long-term impact of heroin on the brain also found some deterioration in white matter, which may impair the ability to make decisions, regulate behavior, and respond to stressful situations.[2] In short, when a drug such as an opioid is ingested, it stimulates the opioid receptors in the brain, and dopamine is released, giving the individual strong feelings of pleasure. This is the same biochemical response that rewards life-sustaining activities such as eating and sex, encouraging the individual to repeat the pleasurable activity. In a similar way, the same reward mechanism "teaches" the individual to repeat the process of creating the high produced by using drugs. Associations may also develop between feeling high and being with people or being in places where the person commonly used drugs. These associations can trigger strong cravings and contribute to relapse at any stage of recovery.

In addition to dulling sensations of physical and emotional pain, opioids can also induce feelings of euphoria, especially when taken at doses higher than prescribed or in a manner other than intended, such as when time-release tablets are crushed to be snorted or injected. Normally, feedback from the prefrontal cortex and other areas in the brain helps an individual overcome the drive for pleasure when it is based on actions that may be unsafe or unwise, but this feedback appears to be compromised in individuals who have become addicted to drugs. Educating patients about the brain changes involved in addiction helps them understand that they are not "bad" or "weak" people, and it can help them move forward more quickly toward initiating positive changes such as understanding the need to practice abstinence.

These neurological changes, along with the changes related to tolerance, dependence, and withdrawal, present significant challenges for people seeking recovery from opioid use disorder. When coupled with potential biological vulnerabilities and environmental stress, individual cases may present even more challenges. Taken together, these brain changes, in addition to associations the opioid user may have developed between drug use and certain settings or people, which can trigger cravings, also present an ongoing risk of relapse at any stage of recovery.

Medication-assisted treatment (MAT) with medications such as methadone, buprenorphine, and naltrexone is effective because these medications act on the same brain structures and processes affected by opioids, but with protective or normalizing effects that make it easier for an individual to participate and engage in treatment programming.[3] Although researchers do not yet know everything about how these medications work, it is clear that along with appropriate psychosocial supports, they are effective parts of a clinical treatment plan, rather than simple substitutes for the illicit opioid.

Effects on the Body

Misuse of opiates, whether prescription painkillers or heroin, can have a very serious negative impact on almost every part of the user's body. The dangers of using heroin or misusing prescription painkillers include sedation, mental confusion, slowing of the digestive system (nausea and constipation), greater pain sensitivity, and depressed respiration,[4] which is of particular concern because it can result in dangerously low levels of blood oxygen, which can result in permanent brain damage or death.[5] In addition, sharing needles used to inject heroin and injecting crushed pills pose their own dangers, including causing veins to collapse, reducing immune response, and contracting diseases like HIV/AIDS or hepatitis B and C—also a risk when engaging in unsafe sex while high. In addition, contamination from heroin or crushed opioid pills can cause a serious infection of the heart lining (endocarditis).

Opioid use in pregnant women is associated with increased odds of threatened preterm labor, early onset delivery, and stillbirth.[6] Most newborns of mothers who used opioids during pregnancy develop symptoms of neonatal abstinence syndrome (NAS), a postnatal drug withdrawal syndrome primarily caused by maternal opioid use.[7] NAS is treatable and has not been associated with long-term adverse consequences.[8]

Opioids are very effective for acute pain, such as that resulting from an accident or following surgery. They are also considered effective in palliative care for terminal conditions such as cancer. However, increased attention is being paid to the long-term use of opioids, meaning use lasting ninety days or more. Addiction is a primary concern in long-term use, but there is also the potential for hyperalgesia, a condition in which pain is worsened or the patient's sensitivity to pain is heightened.[9]

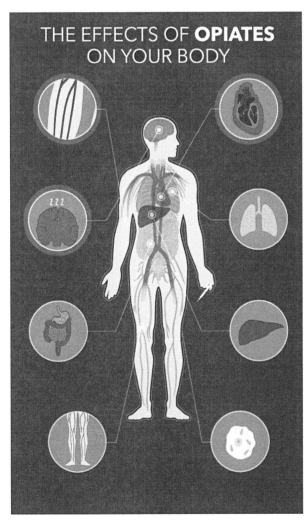

THE EFFECTS OF **OPIATES** ON YOUR BODY

BLOOD
Heroin or crushed-pill injections can cause veins to collapse.

HEART
Heart lining can become infected due to contamination from heroin or crushed pills.

BRAIN
Heavy opiate use can cause sedation.

LUNGS
Ensuing respiratory depression can lead to slowed breathing, which is potentially fatal.

DIGESTIVE SYSTEM
Slowing of the digestive system can result in constipation.

LIVER
Shared infected needles can cause hepatitis.

NERVOUS SYSTEM
Chronic opiate abuse can create a greater sensitivity to pain.

IMMUNE SYSTEM
Vulnerability and infection can occur due to reduced immune response.

Reprinted from https://drugabuse.com/featured/the-effects-of-opiates-on-the-body.

Dependence, Tolerance, and Addiction

Physical dependence on opioids occurs as a result of physiological changes due to prolonged opioid use and means that the body relies on the opioid drug to prevent withdrawal. Physical dependence can be managed with medication and is resolved with a slow taper off the opioid.

Physical dependence can occur without addiction; this can be true of patients who take an opioid medication as prescribed for chronic pain but don't develop the uncontrollable compulsion and loss of control displayed in patients with an opioid use disorder.

Tolerance to opioids occurs when more of the drug is needed to produce the same effect, often after people take opioids for long periods of time. The human body naturally produces its own opioid chemicals (endorphins, enkephalins). But over time, continued use of opioid drugs causes the body to produce smaller amounts of these opioid chemicals (endogenous opioids), resulting in symptoms of withdrawal if drugs are stopped.[10]

The criteria for an addiction (or an opioid use disorder) diagnosis involve changes to the brain and include tolerance, withdrawal, compulsive drug seeking despite negative consequences, cravings, and an inability to control drug use.[11] While the brain abnormalities that produce opioid dependence appear to resolve after detoxification (often within weeks after opioid use stops), the brain abnormalities that produce addiction are more wide-ranging, complex, and long-lasting, affecting the brain's reward system and producing cravings that can lead to relapse months or years after an individual is no longer opioid dependent.

Medical facilities have seen an increase in the number of patients seeking treatment for opioid use disorder (opioid addiction). A Blue Cross Blue Shield analysis of its members found that the number of people diagnosed with an addiction to opioids climbed 493 percent between 2010 and 2016. In 2010, there were 1.4 incidences of opioid use disorder among every 1,000 members. By 2016, that rate had climbed to 8.3 incidences per 1,000 members.[12] This includes people addicted to legal prescription drugs like oxycodone and hydrocodone, as well as illicit drugs such as heroin.

To make a clinical diagnosis of an opioid use disorder (or addiction), providers can refer to the American Psychiatric Association's *Diagnostic and Statistical Manual of Mental Disorders, 5th Edition (DSM-5)*. In this latest edition of *DSM*, the terminology used for addiction disorders has changed. Instead of separating them into categories such as substance abuse, chemical dependency, or addiction, the guide now uses one term—*substance use disorder*—to include the full range of problematic drug use. To be officially diagnosed with a heroin or prescription painkiller problem, someone would be classified as having an opioid use disorder, also some-times referred to in the medical community as an opioid addiction. In this guide, we use the terms *opioid addiction* and *opioid use disorder* interchangeably as a conve-nience to readers, since they are the terms most commonly understood by the gen-eral public.

DSM-5 includes a list of criteria to help behavioral health professionals determine whether a person has a mild, moderate, or severe form of a substance use disorder. Learn more at DSM5.org.

Opioid Withdrawal

Long-term opioid use changes the way nerve cells work in the brain. The nerve cells become accustomed to opioids, and when individuals stop opioid use suddenly, they will experience withdrawal symptoms that may be described as similar to an extremely bad flu virus, with symptoms of body aches, fever, sweating, diarrhea, vomiting, shaking, or chills, as well as anxiety and/or irritability. These symptoms are extremely unpleasant (with some doctors describing patients in withdrawal as being in "terrible misery"). Some symptoms can be longer lasting and can affect cog-nitive ability and mood. Because opioids can profoundly disrupt the reward sys-tem in the human brain, recovery from an opioid use disorder can be challenging with strong to severe symptoms of withdrawal and cravings. MAT can be helpful in addressing both issues for patients who are evaluated and deemed appropriate can-didates for a medication. The use of MAT is covered in detail in Chapter 6: Effective Treatment of Opioid Use Disorder.

Withdrawal from opioids is difficult and lasts longer than withdrawal from many other substances, and it can pose a challenge to effective treatment as these patients often struggle with cravings, impulsivity, limited distress tolerance, sleep issues, chronic pain, poor coping skills, and cognitive difficulties such as problems focusing and remembering. During treatment, the severity of opioid withdrawal may be assessed using the Clinical Opioid Withdrawal Scale (COWS). Nurses should be trained to administer this tool and record their results on a flow sheet so that changes can be tracked easily.

Opioid Overdose

An overdose can occur when a person takes more medication than is prescribed, takes it in a manner other than which it was intended to be taken, or takes too much of an illicit opioid. An overdose can also occur as a result of a lowered tolerance.

Duplicating this page is illegal. Do not duplicate without the publisher's written permission.

17

A person's tolerance falls quickly once he or she discontinues all opioid use. As a result, an overdose can easily occur if a person who had been abstaining from opioid use returns to using his or her normal dose (prior to abstinence), due to lowered tolerance.

Opioids in high doses can cause respiratory depression and death. Because of their capacity to cause respiratory depression, opioids are responsible for a high proportion of fatal drug overdoses around the world.

Combining opioid medications with other drugs can also greatly impact the way either or both substances act on the body. This is particularly true of opioids and other central nervous system depressants, such as alcohol or benzodiazepines.[13] When medications are combined, an overdose can occur even when taking an amount that would be considered safe if the medication were taken by itself. Symptoms of opioid overdose include small ("pinpoint") pupils, slowed or stopped breathing, unresponsiveness, or loss of consciousness. Other symptoms may include a limp body, pale and clammy skin, a purple tint in lips or under fingernails, and vomiting.[14]

According to the CDC, those at the greatest risk for opioid overdose and death include (1) the nearly nine million Americans who report long-term medical use of opioids and (2) the roughly five million who report using opioids without a prescription during the previous month. Also, people with mental disorders are overrepresented among those who get opioid prescriptions and among those who overdose on these drugs.[15]

Most people with a prescription for opioids—about 80 percent—are prescribed low doses by a single practitioner. Another 10 percent of individuals are prescribed higher doses by a single practitioner. The remaining 10 percent are the high-risk individuals who are of greatest concern, because they account for 40 percent of opioid overdoses. These are patients who seek care from multiple doctors, are prescribed high daily doses of opioids, and get opioids from people without a prescription. The CDC recommends that efforts to prevent opioid overdose and death should focus primarily on this high-risk group of patients.[16]

As drug overdose has now surpassed car accidents as the leading cause of accidental death in the United States, with 75 percent of those deaths resulting from opioid overdose, the CDC describes prescription drug overdose as an "epidemic" and "the fastest growing drug problem in the United States."[17] The CDC and the National Institute on Drug Abuse (NIDA) offer statistics about opioid use in particular:

• Nationwide, more than 64,000 people died of a drug overdose in 2016.[18] In 2015, approximately 33,000 overdose deaths were related to opioid use.[19]

- In 2016, more than forty-six people died each day from overdoses involving prescription opioids.[20]
- Overdose deaths involving prescription opioids were five times higher in 2016 than in 1999,[21] and sales of these prescription drugs have quadrupled.[22]
- About one-half of prescription painkiller–related deaths involve at least one other drug, including benzodiazepines, cocaine, and heroin. Alcohol is also involved in many overdose deaths.[23]

Reversing Opioid Overdose with Naloxone/Narcan

Medical management of an opioid overdose is similar whether the opioid that was taken was a legally prescribed painkiller or an illegal drug bought on the street, such as heroin. Naloxone (Narcan) is a medication approved by the U.S. Food and Drug Administration (FDA) to counter the effects of opioids and resuscitate the person who has overdosed. It is a temporary drug that wears off in twenty to ninety minutes. It works by reversing the often-fatal depression of the central nervous system and respiratory system caused by opioids. Naloxone can very quickly restore normal respiration to a person whose breathing has slowed or stopped as a result of overdosing with heroin or prescription opioid pain medications. Due to the short-acting nature of naloxone relative to some opioids, users who have been "reversed" from a state of overdose (with naloxone) can return to overdose once the initial dose of naloxone wears off. Thus, while effective, naloxone administration still requires follow-up with emergency care.

Naloxone is often administered by injection into the muscle or under the skin or sprayed into the nose for absorption into the nasal mucosa. Naloxone is safe to use on pregnant women, giving the lowest dose to avoid acute withdrawal and stress on the fetus. Intranasal naloxone can be administered by minimally trained laypeople.

Many states have either passed or are currently working to pass laws that give police and first responders, and even concerned family members, the ability to carry and administer naloxone when called to a possible overdose situation. Naloxone has no potential for abuse. It is on the World Health Organization Model List of Essential Medicines, the most effective and safe medicines that are an essential part of any health system.[24]

Duplicating this page is illegal. Do not duplicate without the publisher's written permission.

19

3

Opioids in Special Populations

Patients with circumstances or conditions that require special attention include pregnant women, adolescents and young adults, geriatric patients, and patients with medical comorbidities and those with co-occurring mental health disorders. These patients present with unique issues that may require additional training or specialty care in treatment.

Adolescents and Young Adults

Prescription opioids for pain management include medications such as oxycodone and hydrocodone. In 2015, 276,000 adolescents were current nonmedical users of prescription painkillers, with 122,000 having an addiction to prescription painkillers.[1] Still, among teens, both medical and nonmedical use of opioid medications declined in recent years, starting in 2013. Perhaps more troubling, in 2015, an estimated 21,000 adolescents had used heroin in the past year, and an estimated 5,000 were current heroin users. Additionally, an estimated 6,000 adolescents had a heroin use disorder in 2014.[2]

The prescribing rates for prescription opioids among adolescents and young adults nearly doubled from 1994 to 2007.[3] Many teens who misuse opioids started by using prescription painkillers prescribed by their doctor. In 2015, 8 percent of adolescents reported abusing prescription opioids, and the majority of the adolescents had been medically prescribed opioids. Medically prescribed opioid use before high school graduation is associated with a 33 percent increase in risk of future opioid misuse after high school.[4] Adolescents who misuse prescription painkillers may also get the medication from a friend or relative who is unaware of the dangers of nonmedical opioid use. Regional and national studies indicate that lifetime exposure to prescription opioids in medical or nonmedical contexts among U.S. high school students ranges from 22 percent to 45 percent.

Many young people have the erroneous idea that prescription drugs are "safer" than other drugs, such as cocaine or methamphetamine, because they come from a pharmacy. More and more teens who start with pills are quickly progressing to heroin because of its easier availability, lower cost, and higher purity. The longstanding stereotypes about young people who use heroin no longer apply—honor roll students show up in emergency rooms with overdoses, and teens with clean records start stealing from friends and family to fuel their addiction.

Despite the medical effectiveness of prescribed opioids for pain relief, there are growing health concerns about their high abuse potential and the risk that youth will move to heroin as a cheaper, easier-to-acquire alternative. The good news is that community action is working to raise awareness and to encourage educators, parents, health care providers, and law enforcement to work together to stem the growth of opioid abuse and addiction, especially among young people. The goal is to reach a balance between helpful and essential medical use for treating pain while minimizing the potential for misuse and addiction.

Pregnant Women

A 2014 article in the *New York Times* reported a dramatic rise in opioid prescriptions to pregnant women, often for discomfort, back pain, and other symptoms. One study showed that nearly 23 percent of pregnant women enrolled in Medicaid were prescribed an opioid in 2007, up from 18.5 percent in 2000.[5] Of privately insured pregnant women, the number was 14 percent. Since some over-the-counter drugs can be ineffective or harmful to pregnant women, prescription opioids are often the best option to relieve acute pain, but their use must be strictly monitored. The long-term risks are not well understood, but recent research shows a link between first-trimester use and malformations of the spine and brain in the developing fetus. Prolonged use can lead to dependence in both the mother and the infant, causing birth defects or neonatal abstinence syndrome (NAS) in the infant.

Along with recent increases in opioid use in the United States, the incidence of babies born dependent on opioids (NAS) as a result of the mother's opioid use during pregnancy has also increased nearly fivefold between 2000 and 2012.[6]

NAS happens when a baby is exposed to drugs such as heroin, codeine, oxycodone, methadone, or buprenorphine in the womb before birth, which means the baby can experience withdrawal after birth. Symptoms of NAS in the newborn depend on various factors, including the type of drug the mother used, the amount used, the duration it was used, and how the mother's body breaks down the drug.

Pregnant women with opioid use disorders are likely to use multiple substances during pregnancy, including tobacco and alcohol. Infants prenatally exposed to multiple substances are at risk for developing a wide spectrum of physical, emotional, and developmental problems. Exposure to multiple substances can affect an infant's withdrawal symptoms.[7]

Untreated opioid addiction during pregnancy can have negative effects on the fetus. As the level of opioids fluctuates in the blood of mother, the fetus can experience repeated periods of opioid withdrawal. This could cause preterm labor and puts the fetus at risk of inhibited growth, fetal convulsions, and even fetal death.

The use of medication-assisted treatment (MAT) during pregnancy is a recommended best practice for the care of pregnant women with opioid use disorders.[8] Abrupt discontinuation of opioid use during pregnancy can result in premature labor, fetal distress, and miscarriage. Medical withdrawal from opioids should be conducted under the supervision of physicians experienced in perinatal addiction.[9] However, pregnant women who stop using opioids and subsequently relapse are at greater risk of overdose death. There is also an increased risk of harm to the fetus. Because NAS is treatable, MAT is typically recommended instead of withdrawal or abstinence.[10]

To lessen the negative effects of opioid dependence on the fetus, treatment with methadone has been used for pregnant women with opioid use disorder since the 1970s and has been recognized as the standard of care since 1998. Recent evidence suggests that buprenorphine may also be considered as a treatment option. Both methadone and buprenorphine treatment can help to stabilize fetal levels of opioids, reducing fetal withdrawal and improving neonatal outcomes. NAS still occurs in babies whose mothers have received buprenorphine or methadone, but it is less severe than it would be in the absence of treatment.[12]

> To counter misinformation and inaccurate reporting by the popular media about pregnant women and prescription opioid use, researchers and experts released an open letter to the media and policymakers in March 2013 with the following guidelines:
>
> - Newborn babies are *not* born "addicted," and referring to newborns with NAS as "addicted" is inaccurate, incorrect, and highly stigmatizing. Portraying NAS babies as "victims" results in the vilification of their mothers, who are then viewed as perpetrators, and further perpetuates the criminalization of addiction.
>
> - Using pejorative labels such as *oxy babies*, *oxy tots*, *victims*, *tiny addict*, or *born addicted* places these children at substantial risk of stigma and discrimination and can lead to inappropriate child welfare interventions.
>
> - NAS is treatable and has not been associated with long-term adverse consequences.
>
> - Mischaracterizing MAT as harmful and unethical contradicts the efficacy of MAT and discourages the appropriate and federally recommended treatment for opioid use disorder.[11]

Like any medication given during pregnancy, the use of MAT in pregnant women has both risks and benefits to the mother and fetus. Therefore, MAT needs careful consideration by the pregnant women themselves as well as coordination by the providers and agencies that have influence and authority over this population of pregnant women and their infants.[13]

Treating opioid addiction in pregnant women poses unique issues—such as withdrawal, relapse, and use of MAT—that can be best addressed by providers using a coordinated, multisystem approach. With advanced planning to address safe care for mothers and their newborns, unexpected crises at the time of delivery can be prevented. Unfortunately, only a few of the nation's addiction treatment centers offer services tailored to pregnant or postpartum women, according to the Substance Abuse and Mental Health Services Administration (SAMHSA).

Patients with Medical Comorbidities

Patients addicted to opioids who present for treatment often have other comorbid medical problems. Medical complications can result from the toxic effects of the ingredients of the opioid itself, as well as from the way it is administered. The main medical complications are related to injecting heroin (intravenously, intramuscularly, or subcutaneously). The prevalence of infectious diseases, such as HIV/AIDS, hepatitis B and C, tuberculosis, skin and soft tissue infections, and syphilis and other sexually transmitted diseases, is an additional complication. It is important to screen for and manage common comorbid medical conditions as part of addiction treatment. Screening for comorbid health conditions is especially imperative for patients considering the use of MAT for opioid addiction in order to anticipate known and potential drug interactions.

Patients with Co-occurring Mental Health Disorders

Addiction and mental health disorders are identified as separate and distinct issues that can—and often do—occur together. Effective treatment for co-occurring mental health disorders depends on an accurate diagnosis, which can be a highly complex and somewhat subjective process, especially when paired with symptoms from any substance use disorder, including opioid addiction. As reported in Hazelden's Research Update on addiction and mental illness,[14] the prevalence of substance use disorders in the general population is about 16 percent. That nearly doubles to 29 percent for people with mental health disorders. Over 40 percent of opioid-dependent individuals have a co-occurring mental health disorder.[15] The most common are major depressive disorder, anxiety disorders, and bipolar disorder. People with opioid use disorder may also be diagnosed with schizophrenia, attention-deficit/hyperactivity disorder (ADHD), or post-traumatic stress disorder (PTSD).

While there is no conclusive evidence indicating why substance use disorders and mental health disorders co-occur in many people, the Dartmouth Psychiatric Research Center puts forth several theories, including the following:

- Self-medication. People use alcohol or other drugs to "self-medicate" against disturbing symptoms of mental illness.
- Early onset. Certain drugs of abuse (for example, methamphetamine, cocaine, alcohol) may precipitate an earlier onset of mental illness in certain vulnerable individuals.
- Genetic and environmental. Genetic predisposition or environmental factors (poverty, social isolation, or lack of structure, for example) may cause both substance use problems and mental illness.
- Susceptibility. People with mental illnesses may be more susceptible to the harmful effects of alcohol and other drugs.[16]

Co-occurring disorders in people with any substance use disorder can be especially problematic to diagnose, because the presence of one disorder can interfere with diagnosis of the other. For example, a person with alcohol or other drug dependence is likely to manifest problems with depression or anxiety.

When thinking about use of MAT, those patients with co-occurring mental health disorders present more complicated issues in terms of treatment priorities, stabilization concerns, and medication interactions. It is important to note that combining medications used in MAT with anxiety treatment medications can be fatal. This is because some anxiety treatment medications include derivatives of benzodiazepine.

In treating people with mental health disorders and opioid addiction, an integrated treatment approach is best, with a focus on stabilizing symptoms of the co-occurring mental health disorder while providing the patient with a foundation for recovery from opioid addiction.

▩ ▩ ▩

4

Overview of Treatment and Recovery

Opioid use disorders can be successfully treated. Often a variety of treatment methods are needed: intensive inpatient (residential) treatment, outpatient treatment, continuing care, and individual, group, and family therapy. Effective treatment addresses medical, psychological, legal, social, and vocational issues. And as with other substance use disorders, treatment for opioid use disorders works best along with participation in a Twelve Step fellowship, such as Narcotics Anonymous (NA) or Alcoholics Anonymous (AA), or other community support programs.

Many experts (including those at the Hazelden Betty Ford Foundation) now believe that combining these approaches with medication-assisted treatment (MAT) presents the best chance for successful recovery from opioid use disorders. There are multiple paths to recovery, and new treatment options will continually emerge from research and clinical practice. Treatment providers can best serve patients by staying open to innovation.

Access to Treatment

While treatment works, most of those who need treatment for a substance use disorder never receive it. In 2011, 21.6 million persons age twelve or older needed treatment for an illicit drug or alcohol use problem, but only 2.3 million received treatment at a specialty substance treatment facility. Fewer than one in four people with an opioid use disorder received treatment in 2015.[1]

Strategies to reduce this gap in treatment access include achieving insurance parity for financial coverage of treatment services and expansion of Medicare/Medicaid coverage and increased block grant funding, increasing awareness of the effectiveness of treatment for opioid or other substance use disorders, and reducing the stigma of this disease, as well as reducing the stigma that still exists surrounding the use of MAT. It also includes educating primary care providers on effective screening, brief intervention, and referral to treatment (SBIRT) methods, which allow a

Duplicating this page is illegal. Do not duplicate without the publisher's written permission.

27

provider to intervene before serious drug problems develop, identify people in need of treatment, and connect them with appropriate treatment providers.

Many workplaces sponsor employee assistance programs (EAPs) that offer short-term counseling and/or assistance to employees who suspect they or a loved one may have an alcohol or other drug problem. These EAPs can provide links to local treatment resources, including peer support/recovery groups.

In 2017, the federal government formed the President's Commission on Combating Drug Addiction and the Opioid Crisis and allocated billions of dollars to fight the opioid epidemic over the next few years.[2] The 21st Century Cures Act, signed into law by former president Barack Obama in late 2016, gave the Substance Abuse and Mental Health Services Administration (SAMHSA) hundreds of millions of dollars over the next two years to allocate via state-targeted response (STR) grants. SAMHSA's announcement of the 21st Century Cures Act funding focuses on many activities, one of which is MAT for the treatment of opioid use disorders.[3]

Residential and Outpatient Therapy

Residential treatment programs last from a few days to months. Longer programs may include a halfway-house program that helps the person in recovery gradually reintegrate into society. Outpatient programs offer many of the same features as residential treatment but only occur for a few hours each day or a few days a week. This allows the patient to continue to work and return home each night.

Successful treatment outcomes often depend on a person's ability to stay in treatment long enough to reap its full benefits. Each patient is different, and treatment adherence often is affected by many factors: motivation to change drug-using behavior; degree of support from family and friends; and pressure from the criminal justice system, child protection services, employers, or family. Often family and friends can play an important role in motivating individuals with drug problems to enter and stay in treatment. Within a treatment program, successful clinicians can establish a positive, therapeutic relationship with their patients, including building a treatment plan that is developed cooperatively with the patient seeking treatment. It is the responsibility of the clinician to monitor whether the plan is followed and that the treatment expectations are clearly understood by the patient.

After treatment, the provider should ensure a transition to less intensive continuing care, such as an outpatient support group, a sober house, a recovery coach, and similar supports to help individuals initiate their ongoing recovery as they move toward complete self-management. More on this topic is included in Part 2: Clinical Practice.

Treatment in Criminal Justice Populations

It is estimated that about one-half of state and federal prisoners abuse or are addicted to drugs, but relatively few receive treatment while incarcerated. The cost to society of drug abuse is estimated in the billions—the costs from drug-related crime and also the costs to the victims of crime. The cost of treatment is just a fraction of these overall costs to society. Treatment is cost-effective in reducing drug use and bringing about related savings in health care.

MAT for opioid use disorders can be an important component of effective drug abuse treatment for offenders in criminal justice settings. These medications create an environment where the brain can function more normally. This gives the individual the opportunity to focus and engage in treatment programming by reducing the severity of withdrawal and cravings. For example, providing methadone treatment to opioid-addicted prisoners prior to their release not only helps to reduce drug use but also avoids the much higher imprisonment costs for drug-related crime.[4] Although some jurisdictions have found ways to successfully implement MAT for opioid or other substance use disorders, addiction medications are still underused within the criminal justice system, despite evidence of their effectiveness.[5]

Evidence-Based Approaches in Treatment

Some patients and family members may be unaware that evidence-based practices (EBPs) exist in the treatment of substance use disorders. EBPs are treatments that are based on scientific evidence. Most EBPs have been studied in several large-scale clinical trials, involving thousands of patients and careful comparison of the effects of EBPs versus other types of treatments. The approaches listed below are recommended for patients seeking recovery from opioid use disorders and include peer support, behavioral therapy, and MAT.

Cognitive-behavioral therapy (CBT) is used to teach the patient to anticipate common problems in early recovery, identify relapse triggers and ways to address them, recognize and correct distorted thinking processes, and deepen self-control through coping strategies.

Motivational enhancement therapy (MET) focuses on empathic communication to address barriers and build the patient's motivation to change his or her maladaptive behaviors.

Twelve Step Facilitation (TSF) promotes abstinence through patient engagement with Twelve Step fellowship groups, such as AA or NA, and teaching the concepts of the Twelve Steps, such as acceptance, surrender to a Higher Power, and helping others.

Community reinforcement encourages the patient to make positive changes to his or her lifestyle (recreational, familial, social, and vocational) so that healthy, drug-free living becomes more rewarding than continued substance use.

Contingency management reinforces desirable behaviors by applying incentives (such as stickers, medallions, cash, or other rewards) for meeting specific behavioral criteria (such as meeting required treatment appointments or maintaining abstinence as verified by urinalysis).

Medication-assisted treatment (MAT) is another evidence-based practice that is growing in use for treatment of substance use disorders, including alcohol use disorders and opioid use disorders. MAT for opioid use disorders combines behavioral therapy and the use of Federal Drug Administration (FDA)-approved medications including buprenorphine, buprenorphine/naloxone, naltrexone, and methadone. Research has shown that MAT, in conjunction with counseling, is an effective component of effective treatment in people with opioid use disorder.

Some people in the recovery community still believe that using these medications means that they are not being completely abstinent (or drug free) and that they are, in essence, trading one drug addiction for another. However, SAMHSA says that the use of MAT in combination with psychosocial evidence-based therapies (such as CBT and MET) is effective in the treatment of addiction, as it helps patients manage their withdrawal and cravings so they can better engage in and complete treatment.[6]

More about these commonly used evidence-based approaches is found in this guide in Chapter 6: Effective Treatment of Opioid Use Disorder. More about the use of MAT is covered in detail in Chapter 7: Medications Used to Treat Opioid Use Disorder and Chapter 8: MAT as an Integrated Evidence-Based Practice.

■ ■ ■

Part 2

Clinical Practice

5

Screening and Evaluation

Opioid use disorder kills hundreds of Americans each week, despite the availability of treatments that can dramatically reduce mortality risk. There is a lot that providers can do to help these vulnerable patients, including identifying patients who need help and getting them to a provider who meets their needs. They can do this through effective screening, brief intervention, and referral to treatment.

Screening, brief intervention, and referral to treatment (SBIRT) is an evidence-based practice that involves screening people for risky substance use, briefly intervening with motivational interviewing techniques to raise awareness of the consequences of continued use and to incentivize positive change, and referring high-risk individuals to further assessment and specialty treatment.

It's important to be able to quickly recognize the signs of opioid misuse and opioid use disorder in patients. Some opioid users are able to carry on their addiction for a long time without showing outward signs that anything is wrong. As a provider, if you suspect an opioid use disorder, you can be a powerful influence to get a patient to seek help. Primary care physicians are often the first health care provider to become aware of a patient's substance use disorder, and they have a responsibility to refer a patient to treatment.

If opioid misuse is left untreated, the consequence for some patients can be dire. Recent statistics suggest that all too often, a patient who is addicted to prescription pain medication moves on to nonmedical use of opioids and heroin. Many patients who struggle with addiction begin their drug use with prescription opioids and swear they would never use a needle or heroin. They often surprise themselves by eventually making the switch once they can no longer afford prescriptions, have shopped on the illegal drug market, and struggle with withdrawal symptoms.

Diagnostic Methods

The American Psychiatric Association's *Diagnostic and Statistical Manual of Mental Disorders, 5th Edition (DSM-5)* is a manual used by behavioral health professionals,

Duplicating this page is illegal. Do not duplicate without the publisher's written permission.

33

such as psychiatrists and psychologists, as a guide to diagnosing people with sub-stance use and mental health disorders. As noted in Part 1 of this guide, *DSM-5* has modified the terminology used for addiction disorders. Instead of separating such problems into categories such as substance abuse, chemical dependency, or addic-tion, the guide now uses one term—*substance use disorder*—to include the full range of problematic drug use. Individuals with addiction to opioids such as heroin or pre-scription painkillers are classified as having an opioid use disorder.

In the paragraphs that follow, we present the difference between opioid depen-dence, tolerance, and addiction.

When creating a clinical diagnosis, please consult *DSM-5* for a current list of criteria that providers can use to determine whether a person has a mild, moderate, or severe form of opioid use disorder. Learn more at DSM5.org.

Dependence, Tolerance, and Addiction

There are a variety of terms used to describe opioid use disorders. Each of these terms can mean different things to different people, making it important to adopt specific definitions so a clear discussion of these disorders can be held.

Nonmedical use of opioids refers to an individual using a prescription pain reliever even once that was not prescribed for that individual, or if the opioid was taken by the individual only for the experience or feeling it caused.[1]

Misuse of opioids refers to an individual's incorrect use of an opioid medication. This includes any of the following:

• using the medication for other than its prescribed purpose
• taking more than the prescribed amount of the medication
• taking the medication more frequently or for longer than prescribed[2]

Physical dependence to opioids occurs as a result of physiological changes due to prolonged opioid use and means that the body relies on the opioid drug to prevent withdrawal. Physical dependence can be managed with medication and is resolved with a slow taper off the opioid. Physical dependence can occur without addiction; this can be true of patients who take an opioid medication as prescribed for chronic pain but don't develop the uncontrollable compulsion and loss of control displayed in patients with an opioid use disorder.

Tolerance to opioids occurs when more of the drug is needed to produce the same effect. Tolerance occurs when people take opioids for long periods of time. The human body naturally produces its own opioid chemicals (endorphins, enkephalins).

Over time, continued use of opioid drugs causes the body to produce smaller amounts of these opioid chemicals (endogenous opioids), resulting in symptoms of withdrawal if drugs are stopped.[3]

Addiction (or opioid use disorder) diagnosis criteria involve changes to the brain and include tolerance, withdrawal, compulsive drug seeking despite negative consequences, cravings, and an inability to control drug use.[4] While the abnormalities that produce opioid dependence appear to resolve after detoxification (often within weeks after opioid use stops), the abnormalities that produce addiction are more wide-ranging, complex, and long-lasting, affecting the brain's reward system and producing cravings that can lead to relapse months or years after an individual is no longer opioid dependent.

The American Society of Addiction Medicine (ASAM) defines *addiction,* or *substance dependence,* as "a primary, chronic disease of brain reward, motivation, memory and related circuitry."[5] The following are key signs of any addiction (including addiction to opioids):

- inability to control drug use
- compulsive drug use
- continued drug use despite harm
- cravings for the drug[6]

Screening in Primary Care Settings

Depending on the setting, primary care physicians may encounter patients seeking help for pain from surgery, illness, or injury who are not yet taking opioids. They may also encounter patients taking high doses of opioids who have some level of opioid use disorder and may be in opiate withdrawal or even overdose.

For patients not yet taking an opioid who need pain management, it's highly recommended that a primary care physician screen these patients before starting them on prescription opioids. There are screening tools designed for physicians to assess risk for opioid misuse among individuals who have not yet started taking prescribed opioids for treatment of chronic pain. The Opioid Risk Tool (ORT) is a brief self-report screening tool designed for this purpose. Given the harsh consequences of potential opioid misuse, early screening and monitoring when prescribing opioids is critical.

In 2016, the Centers for Disease Control and Prevention (CDC) introduced a document entitled "Guideline for Prescribing Opioids for Chronic Pain." It contains recommendations on items providers should discuss with patients about the risks and benefits of opioid therapy for chronic pain, how to improve the safety and effectiveness of pain treatment, and how to reduce the risks associated with long-term opioid therapy, including opioid use disorder and overdose. The guideline includes suggestions such as discussing benefits and risks, starting opioid therapy with the lowest effective dosage, establishing measurable treatment goals related to pain and others, re-evaluating patients (conducting a risk/benefit analysis) a minimum of every three months, and more. Refer to the full "Guideline for Prescribing Opioids for Chronic Pain" for more information.[7]

For patients who must continue to take prescription opioids for pain for extended periods of time, there are screening tools that can be used periodically to assess their ongoing risk for opioid misuse. This includes the Current Opioid Misuse Measure (COMM), as well as the Screener and Opioid Assessment for Patients with Pain (SOAPP) tool, which physicians can use to predict possible opioid misuse in chronic pain patients and to determine how much monitoring a patient on long-term opioid therapy might require.

Patients with existing substance use disorders and those with a family history of addiction are at a high risk for opioid misuse. When treating these patients for chronic pain, opioids should be avoided if at all possible. Begin with a nonaddictive medication, using alternative and complementary therapies. Most likely, these patients will need to be referred to a pain specialist, addiction specialist, or clinic. If opioids have to be used to treat acute pain, such as post-operative pain, have a frank discussion about risk for relapse, limits on medications, and a strict dosing schedule with no refills until the patient is re-evaluated. You might suggest that a family member or trusted friend "hold" the medication for the patient and only dispense the needed amount, one day at a time.

Primary care physicians should routinely screen all patients for potential alcohol or substance use disorders. If a physician uses a brief screening instrument and finds that the patient is likely to have an opioid use disorder, then a more detailed assessment should follow to create a diagnosis. There are common screening tools to identify whether a patient has a problem with alcohol or other drugs, including opioids. These include tools such as the CAGE questionnaire, the National Institute on Drug Abuse Drug Screening Tool, the Drug Abuse Screening Test (DAST), and others. These screening tools are commonly used in addiction treatment settings as well as primary care settings. A list of screening, assessment, and diagnostic tools is included in Appendix A of this guide.

In discussions with a physician, a patient may not initially feel comfortable disclosing his or her opioid or other drug use because of stigma or shame about his or her opiate use, worry about the pain of opiate withdrawal, and fear of loss of access to prescription pain medication. Physicians may find patients are more willing to disclose drug use when the physician approaches them in an honest, respectful, matter-of-fact way—just as they would when screening for other health disorders. If screening indicates the patient may have an opioid use disorder, the patient should be thoroughly assessed to verify a diagnosis and determine the appropriate treatment setting.

Assessment

The assessment process is similar, whether in a primary care setting or in an addiction treatment setting. Individuals who screen positive for a potential opioid use disorder receive an in-depth assessment to verify a diagnosis, determine readiness for change, and develop specific treatment recommendations. Patients need an immediate assessment of vital signs and labs to establish current drug use (drug use test, blood alcohol level test, and others). Signs of opioid intoxication include drooping eyelids, constricted (pinpoint) pupils, reduced respiratory rate, scratching (from histamine release), and head nodding. During the assessment, a nurse or similar provider looks for critical issues that call for immediate intervention. In patients who have recently used opioids, it is especially important to monitor their respiratory rate due to the risk of respiratory depression. Oxygen saturation may be assessed at the bedside using a finger oximeter. Examples of critical issues could include extreme intoxication that may be life threatening, belligerent behaviors, withdrawal symptoms, suicidal ideation, or psychosis.

The assessment process includes a physical examination to identify opioid intoxication, withdrawal, or overdose and to identify comorbid medical conditions. The main medical complications (HIV, hepatitis B and C, tuberculosis, and syphilis) are related to injecting heroin. Patients with opioid use disorder often have comorbid medical conditions that can complicate their treatment and may require transfer to a higher level of care. The assessment should also include a complete health history and relevant lab tests (pregnancy test, toxicology test, HIV antibody test, and mental health examination or psychiatric assessment, as indicated). The assessment includes a history of past drug use patterns and evaluation of vulnerability to relapse, which is vital to tailoring a treatment plan to best fit the patient's individual needs.

A mental health professional often also conducts a thorough initial mental health assessment. This is important for assessing risk as well as determining the need for mental health services—suicide and self-harm are prime concerns for patients entering treatment. This assessment includes a psychosocial history with a strong emphasis on the patient's mental health history, current mental health status, medications, and the need for further assessment by a psychiatrist. The mental health professional also designs relevant treatment plans, assigns the patient to specific mental health groups, schedules individual sessions when necessary, and determines whether further psychological testing is needed.

Brief Intervention

Brief intervention is a patient-centered strategy that uses a short five- to ten-minute discussion aimed at changing a patient's behavior by increasing insight and awareness regarding substance use. The discussion provides the patient with personalized feedback that shows concern about the consequences of his or her continued drug use. Frequently addressed topics include how substances, such as opioids and others, can cause dangerous interactions with other medications, cause or exacerbate health problems, or interfere with personal responsibilities. It often is used to encourage a patient to decrease or abstain from using the drug. The patient is encouraged to discuss likes and dislikes and consequences related to using the opioid (whether prescription medication or illicit opioid), and how he or she may consider changing behavior.

A more intensive intervention may be used with moderate- to high-risk patients with an opioid use disorder. This intervention often consists of multiple sessions to educate and motivate the patient to move away from harmful and dangerous drug-related behavior (including harmful injection practices) and toward healthy change. Motivational interviewing (MI) techniques are used to help patients discuss the positive and negative effects of opioid use and connect that use with problems they are experiencing in their life. This may include problems with family, parenting, school or work, physical health, and many others. During the conversation, the patient will examine how ready he or she is to reduce or completely abstain from opioid use. If the patient is ready to change, a treatment plan and reasonable goals are set. If the patient is a good candidate for medication-assisted treatment (MAT), this is part of the treatment planning discussion. The flow of the intensive intervention can be flexible to approach the patient "where they are at in that point in time." A provider can often move the patient upward through the stages of change by collaborating on a treatment plan that is tailored to the patient's specific goals: for example, completing college, retaining a job, or healing family matters.

Evaluating Medication Pathways

Evaluating a patient for MAT best begins during the clinical assessment process and benefits from input from a multidisciplinary treatment team, including the patient, a mental health professional, the alcohol and drug counselor, physicians, and other third-party stakeholders, such as family members or criminal justice staff. This team can collaborate to evaluate the medication options that can be presented to the patient for selection. Psychiatry, wellness, spiritual care, and nutritional specialists may also be consulted based on a patient's needs. These roles will vary greatly from one treatment organization to another, depending on the scope and staffing patterns of the treatment program.

All medication pathway options should be discussed, including using no medication at all or using a medication such as buprenorphine/naloxone, naltrexone, or methadone. During this evaluation for MAT, the team will consider the patient's needs along with any medical indications or contraindications.

Factors impacting the decision to utilize MAT for a patient generally include answers to these questions:

- Does the patient have any medical contraindications, such as significant liver or respiratory disease, that preclude the use of MAT?
- Does the patient have a history of an alcohol or other sedative use disorder that could cause significant sedation if used with a medication such as buprenorphine/naloxone?
- Does the patient have insurance or other financial resources to cover the cost of continuing care and medications?
- Is the patient willing and able to meet the requirements for MAT—attending appointments and groups, taking medications as prescribed, and having regular urine drug screens?
- Is the patient willing and able to identify a support person and sign releases to that person?

Medications for the treatment of opioid use disorder should be prescribed as part of a comprehensive individualized treatment plan that includes counseling and other psychosocial therapies, as well as social support through participation in Narcotics Anonymous (NA) and other mutual-help programs.

Referral to Treatment

For primary care providers, referral to treatment allows clinicians to connect those in need of services with a suitable treatment provider that can meet the substance use, medical and mental health, social, and financial needs of the patient.

Referrals are better facilitated when the primary care provider is informed about effective treatment options and facilities that can best treat patients with opioid use disorders. For best outcomes, the patient should be collaboratively involved in the process. Ask: Is the patient ready to address his or her opioid use disorder? Is the patient a candidate for the use of MAT, such as buprenorphine or buprenorphine/

naloxone? Does our health agency offer the needed treatment, including MAT? If not, identify suitable referral options.

Primary care providers should refer the patient for more intensive or specialized services if the agency does not have the resources to meet a particular patient's needs. Providers can find programs in their areas or throughout the United States by using the Substance Abuse and Mental Health Services Administration (SAMHSA) Behavioral Health Treatment Services Locator at www.findtreatment .samhsa.gov. This directory also offers a list of providers specifically authorized to provide buprenorphine treatment for opioid dependency.

In assessing a potential referral, verify that the patient has financial support and/or insurance coverage for the treatment facility. To make an effective referral, include the patient in the process of evaluating potential referral treatment facilities, engaging him or her in conversations about any barriers that might hinder access to following up on the referral. This includes making sure the patient has transportation to the referral site and arrives as planned.

The absence of a proper treatment referral can prevent the patient from receiving timely and appropriate care, can exacerbate other health issues, and drives up the overall cost of care.

The following four steps cover the basics of referral to treatment:

1. Determine the patient's specific needs (are there other comorbid physical or mental health issues, will MAT likely be used, and is inpatient or outpatient care best for this patient?).
2. Identify referral options (keep in mind location, level of care, and financial or other barriers).
3. Make an effective referral (engage the patient in the process and plan to address any identified barriers).
4. Document and follow up with the referral source and patient (ensure documentation exchange and make sure the patient arrived safely and needs are being addressed).

Clinical documentation about the referral ensures that funding, regulatory, and legal requirements of collecting patient mental health and substance use information are met. The provider making the referral will need to obtain standard treatment consent forms and feedback form/service authorizations exchanged between external referral sources.

Primary legal issues to consider include the Health Insurance Portability and Accountability Act (HIPAA) and the Code of Federal Regulations, Title 42 (42 CFR).

HIPAA regulations protect a patient's health information and govern the way providers and benefit plans collect, maintain, use, and disclose protected health information. 42 CFR is designed to ensure that a patient seeking or using services for alcohol or drug use is not made more vulnerable due to the availability of his or her medical record. HIPAA allows, but does not require, programs to make disclosures to other health care providers without authorization, while 42 CFR prohibits disclosure unless there is authorization, there is a court order, or the disclosure is done without revealing personal information. Most health organizations address these regulations by using standard treatment consent forms and feedback form/service authorizations within their agency and between external referral sources.

Treatment of Opioid Use Disorder in the Primary Care Setting

As discussed earlier in this guide, the opioid epidemic is undeniably our nation's fastest-growing public health crisis. Between 1993 and 2012, the hospitalization rate for overuse of opioids—prescription painkillers such as morphine, codeine, fentanyl, and oxycodone—has more than doubled, according to research from the Agency for Healthcare Research and Quality (AHRQ). Hospitalization rates for overuse of opioid pain medications is climbing among every adult age group and in every region of the country, although hospitalizations increased most dramatically in Georgia, where rates increased a whopping 99 percent between 2009 and 2014.[8] This growing opioid-related health crisis has put a huge strain on our health care system. Primary care physicians are uniquely positioned to recognize patient problems with opioids and treat or refer patients before it's too late.

To expand access to addiction treatment, the Drug Addiction Treatment Act of 2000 allowed physicians to treat opioid dependence in their own practices with Schedule III, IV, or V opioid medications that have been approved by the FDA for opioid treatment. In 2002, this included using the prescription medication buprenorphine and the abuse-deterrent formulation of buprenorphine/naloxone.[9] Physicians must take and pass a certifying course (available through ASAM) and then must apply for a special waiver allowing them to treat opioid addiction with the above-mentioned medications.

Certified providers are allowed to provide treatment and services in a range of settings, including hospitals, correctional facilities, offices, and remote clinics. They must provide medical, counseling, vocational, educational, and other assessment and treatment services, in addition to prescribed medication, such as buprenorphine, for opioid use disorder. This is because treatment of opioid addiction with buprenorphine is most effective in combination with behavioral therapy, such as cognitive-behavioral therapy (CBT), and self-help programs, such as peer support and the Twelve Step model of recovery. Learn more about the physician certification requirements at SAMHSA.gov.

Despite the scale of this crisis and despite the fact that physicians report that buprenorphine treatment can result in an 80 percent reduction in illicit opioid use, very few primary care doctors report treating opioid use disorders.[10] A recent study shows that even physicians who have completed the training to receive the waiver rarely prescribe buprenorphine to patients. Primary care providers who don't treat opioid use disorder can refer patients to addiction treatment centers or to another local certified opioid treatment program.

Treatment of Opioid Use Disorder with an Addiction Treatment Provider

Specialized, advanced addiction treatment facilities, such as the Hazelden Betty Ford Foundation, are uniquely poised to handle the complex needs of individuals needing treatment for opioid use disorder. Treatment (covered in detail in Chapter 6: Effective Treatment of Opioid Use Disorder) is available in variety of comprehensive treatment options, including inpatient and outpatient addiction treatment programs.

MAT may or may not be a part of each treatment option, depending on patient needs. In essence, MAT is not the use of medications alone, but instead is the use of prescribed medications in combination with other evidence-based interventions or therapies to promote long-term recovery from opioid use disorders. A good model followed by the Hazelden Betty Ford Foundation combines evidence-based models of psychosocial therapy and peer support along with medications for treatment of opioid use disorder—and uses these elements in a way tailored to the needs of the patient and his or her unique challenges and clinical severity. This model offers patients the best chance at successful recovery from opioid use disorder.

■ ■ ■

6

Effective Treatment of Opioid Use Disorder

Treatment is one light at the end of the very dark tunnel of opioid addiction. Treatment does work, and it is a wise investment. Every dollar spent on treatment saves up to twelve dollars in health, social, and criminal justice costs.[1] Many people need treatment for opioid use disorders, but treatment must work within constraints of finances, facility/location, and other patient needs, responsibilities, and schedules. Individuals progress through drug addiction treatment at various rates, so there is no predetermined length of treatment, as this often depends on the patient's clinical need, insurance coverage, and financial resources. The provider's responsibility is to determine and offer clinically appropriate treatment at the lowest level of care possible first, per the American Society of Addiction Medicine (ASAM) Criteria for choosing a level of care for treating substance use disorders.[2] More severe patients at high relapse risk are appropriate for inpatient treatment only, while other patients with lower relapse risk and higher levels of family involvement and support may be appropriate for outpatient treatment.

Residential treatment programs can last from a few days to months, and they are well suited to patients in opioid recovery, as the inpatient setting offers better 24/7 medical support for withdrawal and initiation of medication-assisted treatment (MAT) to assist with withdrawal and cravings, as opposed to outpatient treatment, where patients spend less time in a supervised environment with providers.

Many outpatient programs offer similar features as residential treatment programs but at a lower level of care, as outpatient services can occur in models that include six to twelve hours of service per week all the way up to twenty-five hours of care per week. These different outpatient offerings can match the patient's clinical needs while often allowing the patient to continue to go to work or school and return home each night.

Living arrangements are a critical part of outpatient care. Patients with opioid use disorders are at high risk for environmentally triggered relapse in early recovery. Engagement in a clean and sober living arrangement is essential and can range from including a very high level of care to being less structured. The highest level of support is found in supported recovery housing (SRH), where patients live on campus with medical, mental health, and addiction staff support 24/7, and which is often linked to emergency services in the community. Less structured options include living in sober housing in the community, and the least structured option is living at home with family or friends. Decisions on housing should be based on the treatment facility's capacity for housing support and its ability to provide the patient a safe place to stay at this critical time.

Evidence-Based Practices

The following table[3] provides a brief overview of commonly used evidence-based approaches for the treatment of substance use disorders. These include cognitive-behavioral therapy, motivational enhancement therapy including motivational interviewing, Twelve Step Facilitation, community reinforcement, contingency management, and medication-assisted treatment.

These therapies range from a focus on the patients' motivation to change their substance use behaviors, to helping them see inaccuracies in how they process information about their environment, to increasing their understanding of spirituality and stressing the importance of Twelve Step meeting attendance in supporting recovery. Any of these approaches can be included in the treatment of opioid use disorder.

Commonly used evidence-based approaches for the treatment of substance use disorders include cognitive-behavioral therapy, motivational enhancement therapy, Twelve Step Facilitation, community reinforcement, contingency management, and medication-assisted treatment.

TABLE 1

Evidence-Based Practices in Treatment of Substance Use Disorders

Approach	Clinical focus	Settings
Cognitive-behavioral therapy	Teaching the patient to anticipate problems/ risks to relapse and how to address them, recognizing distorted thinking processes and how to correct them, enhancing self-control through coping strategies	Addiction treatment programs, mental health programs/providers
Motivational enhancement therapy	Addressing barriers in the patient's motivation to change maladaptive behaviors, eliciting rapid and internally motivated change, focusing on empathic communication	Addiction treatment programs, mental health programs/providers
Twelve Step Facilitation	Promoting abstinence through facilitating patient engagement with Twelve Step fellowship groups like AA and NA; teaching the concepts of acceptance, surrender to a Higher Power, and the importance of helping others	Addiction treatment programs
Community reinforcement	Eliminating positive reinforcement for using drugs and increasing positive reinforcement for abstinence, teaching new coping behaviors for high-risk situations, focusing on involving significant others in the recovery process	Addiction treatment programs
Contingency management	Grounded in learning theory, involving applying non-drug-related reinforcers to increase abstinence	Addiction treatment programs, mental health programs/providers, primary care settings
Medication-assisted treatment	Using prescribed medications in combination with other evidence-based therapies (including appropriate psychosocial supports). These medications work by reducing withdrawal and cravings, making it easier for the patient to maintain abstinence.	Addiction treatment programs, mental health programs/providers, primary care settings

Cognitive-Behavioral Therapy

Cognitive-behavioral therapy (CBT) is a technique that examines the interactions between a patient's *thoughts* (cognition) and *behavior*. CBT was developed by Aaron Beck, MD, an American psychiatrist at the University of Pennsylvania. This cognitive therapy developed from work with depressed patients who experienced cognitive distortions as a result of their poor mood. For example, a depressed patient may state, "I'm never going to feel better, so what is the point?" The therapist might examine whether the person has ever felt better after an episode of depression (which most patients have) to demonstrate the overgeneralization of this thought process. In this case, CBT helps the patient understand how distorted thinking affects mood and behavior.

For substance use disorder treatment with CBT, thoughts and emotional states that lead to substance use are discussed by the therapist and patient. Understanding these triggers allows patients to make plans for avoiding relapse, either by avoiding these triggers or changing their response to triggers when they occur.

Motivational Interviewing and Motivational Enhancement Therapy

Motivational interviewing (MI) is a style of patient interaction developed by William Miller and Stephen Rollnick. MI is a goal-oriented, patient-centered method a counselor can use to drive positive behavior change in patients by using affirmations, open-ended questions, and reflective listening while asking them to explore and resolve their resistance to change. MI is designed both to enhance the therapeutic relationship and to help the patient become more willing to participate in the change process, to take responsibility, and to move more successfully through the stages of change (precontemplation, contemplation, preparation, action, and maintenance).

MI has proven successful in helping providers engage and retain patients in treatment for substance use disorders.[4] The approach chosen should communicate to patients that the therapist really is interested in them as a person and truly cares about helping them help themselves. Therapists should be trained to learn how to create this change-friendly, nurturing environment.

Motivational enhancement therapy (MET), based on the principles of motivational interviewing, is a counseling approach that helps a patient resolve his or her ambivalence about engaging in treatment and stopping drug use by improving his or her motivation to change.

Twelve Step Facilitation

Twelve Step Facilitation (TSF) therapy is an active engagement strategy designed to increase the likelihood of a person with a substance use disorder becoming affiliated with and actively involved in Twelve Step self-help groups, thereby promoting abstinence. The Twelve Steps practice three key ideas: (1) acceptance, which includes the realization that drug addiction is a chronic, progressive disease over which one has no control, that life has become unmanageable because of drugs, that willpower alone is insufficient to overcome the problem, and that abstinence is the only alternative; (2) surrender, which involves giving oneself over to a Higher Power, accepting the fellowship and support structure of other recovering addicted individuals, and following the recovery activities laid out by the Twelve Step program; and (3) active involvement in Twelve Step meetings and related activities. While the efficacy of Twelve Step programs (and Twelve Step Facilitation) in treating alcohol dependence has been established, the research on its usefulness for other forms of substance use is more preliminary, but the treatment appears promising for helping people who use substances other than alcohol to sustain recovery.[5]

Community Reinforcement

The community reinforcement approach (CRA) has been successfully used to treat a variety of substance use disorders.[6] CRA helps people make positive changes to their lifestyles (recreational, familial, social, and vocational) so that healthy, drug-free living becomes more rewarding than continued alcohol or other drug use. At the core of CRA is the belief that an individual's environment (community) can play a powerful role in encouraging or discouraging drug use.

Contingency Management

A large amount of research supports the efficacy of contingency management (CM) for addiction treatment.[7] CM reinforces desirable behaviors by providing incentives for meeting specific behavioral criteria, such as drug-free urine results or attendance at treatment sessions. Incentives may include items with monetary value ranging from as little as one dollar to as much as several hundred dollars. An extensive body of research supports CM's efficacy in treating various behavioral disorders, including alcohol use disorder, by reducing drinking and increasing treatment compliance.[8] Reinforcing compliance with treatment-related activities may encourage patients to acquire new skills and overcome psychosocial difficulties associated with their abuse of alcohol or other drugs. While CM has been shown to be effective during treatment, some researchers have questioned whether there is any long-term benefit to CM following treatment.[9]

Medication-Assisted Treatment

Because opioid addictions are so powerful, and because the risk of overdosing after relapse is so high, many people and organizations in the medical community are embracing medication-assisted treatment (MAT) to treat patients with opioid use disorder. Starting in 2015, the White House's National Drug Control Strategy established that a central, effective component for treating people with opioid use disorder is the use of medication in conjunction with counseling. The White House's strategy includes the use of several FDA-approved medications, including buprenorphine, naltrexone, and methadone.

Duplicating this page is illegal. Do not duplicate without the publisher's written permission.

47

At the doses prescribed, these medications do not produce a euphoric "high" but instead minimize withdrawal symptoms and cravings, making it possible for patients to function more normally, attend school or work, and better engage in treatment lessons and learn the skills that will help them manage their ongoing recovery. The ultimate goal may be to eventually wean the patient off the medication, and this may take months or years for some patients. The patient and treatment provider should make this decision together, as tapering the medication must be done gradually and with clinical supervision. In cases of serious and long-term opioid use disorder, a patient may need to take the medication indefinitely.

It's important to remember that medications are only part of an MAT approach. In true medication-assisted treatment, the medications are "assisting" other components of treatment, including a variety of evidence-based psychosocial approaches that address the nonbiological aspects of the opioid use disorder. These include a person's behavior, emotions, thought processes, and interactions within social environments.[10]

More about the use of MAT is covered in detail in Chapter 7: Medications Used to Treat Opioid Use Disorder and Chapter 8: MAT as an Integrated Evidence-Based Practice.

Initiating Treatment

This section covers detoxification or buprenorphine induction, entering the treatment program and preparing to participate in a structured schedule (group therapy, regular individual therapy with an alcohol and drug counselor, and other planned treatment activities), and length of stay.

Induction or Detoxification

As discussed in the previous chapter, treatment begins with a detailed medical screening and assessment before the patient starts treatment programming. The assessment will result in choices for the patient regarding medications utilized, if any, and will determine the path for induction or detoxification.

Patients are typically started on agonist or partial agonist treatments in an outpatient setting, but residential structure can assist with treatment retention while patients get through this process. It is important that medical managed withdrawal (detoxification) from opioids be completed at least seven to ten days before extended-release injectable naltrexone is initiated or resumed.[11] Oftentimes, patients are provided oral naltrexone to ensure that they can tolerate the extended-release formulation.

Patients need to be in the early stages of opioid withdrawal to start treatment with agonist or partial agonist medications. Opioid withdrawal may occur if opioids are stopped abruptly or the dose is reduced substantially. Withdrawal from short-acting opioids usually begins six to twelve hours after the last opioid dose, peaks within thirty-six to seventy-two hours, and often subsides over seven to ten days. Withdrawal from long-acting opioids may begin twenty-four to forty-eight hours after the last dose, may peak at seventy-two to ninety-six hours, and can last for up to several weeks.[12] Symptoms of opioid withdrawal can include anxiety, insomnia, abdominal cramps, nausea and vomiting, diarrhea, myalgia, bone pain, tachycardia, hypertension, hyperthermia, diaphoresis, lacrimation, rhinorrhea, piloerection, mydriasis, yawning, and hyperreflexia.[13] Concurrent withdrawal from other substances, particularly alcohol and benzodiazepines, can be life threatening, and vigilance for detecting such withdrawal is therefore important. The induction process can take some time, as patients must be observed after initial dosing to ensure their safety.

An accurate history of the type of opioid used and administration route, as well as the time of the last dose, is critical in order to anticipate when and if opioid withdrawal is expected. It is common for patients to undergo urine drug testing on admission to accurately document the use of substances other than what the patient has reported. During this initial assessment, the counselor verifies and documents the diagnosis of opioid use disorder, identifies key issues related to the dimensions of the ASAM Criteria, and reviews the patient's medical records obtained from other providers during the preadmission process.

During assessment and continuing in treatment, the severity of opioid withdrawal can be assessed with a tool such as the Clinical Opioid Withdrawal Scale (COWS), the Subjective Opioid Withdrawal Scale (SOWS), or the Objective Opioid Withdrawal Scale (OOWS). Providers should be trained to administer one of these tools and record their results on a flow sheet so that changes can be tracked easily.

Information on using medications to ease withdrawal can be found in Chapter 7: Medications Used to Treat Opioid Use Disorder.

Beginning Psychosocial Programming

After initial assessments are complete and induction or detoxification has been initiated, patients are integrated into their treatment groups. The goal is to move patients into programming as soon as possible to take advantage of the therapeutic benefits of connecting with other patients and their clinical team and participating in a structured schedule. Patients begin group therapy, regular individual therapy with their counselor, connection with peer supports, and other planned treatment

Duplicating this page is illegal. Do not duplicate without the publisher's written permission.

49

activities. Their counselor also gives them a realistic and individualized treatment plan with assignments that promote engagement, hope, and behavioral interventions to increase the likelihood of retention in treatment. Early in the treatment process, staff also introduce the importance of continuing care to establish long-term recovery.

Patients benefit from an orientation to the full range of recovery resources beyond treatment, including, but not limited to, follow-up medical and mental health services, continuing care services, Twelve Step fellowships and other community-based support groups, and recovery housing options. After initiation of programming, patients are encouraged to develop meaningful relationships with their peers, as this is a key therapeutic resource that supports patients with an opioid use disorder through tough times in early treatment and recovery. During treatment, weekly participation in an opioid-specific support group is very helpful for all patients with opioid use disorders. The group offers a supportive, facilitated environment where patients with opioid use disorders can learn from each other, and those using MAT can share experiences or concerns about taking a medication such as buprenorphine/naloxone or naltrexone and offer suggestions about how to face common challenges in early recovery, such as managing withdrawal symptoms, participating openly in Twelve Step recovery meetings, and coping with the severe cravings that often are present in early recovery from opioid use disorders.

Treatment Engagement

Many patients with opioid use disorders have had multiple treatments with limited success at sustaining recovery, protracted withdrawal complications, significant unresolved co-occurring mental health issues, limited coping and recovery skills, and difficult home environment situations with multiple relapse triggers that require intensive case management and clinical services. What is clinically ideal for a patient may not be possible because of insurance, vocational, child care, transportation, and funding issues.

Common Treatment Challenges and Concerns

This section covers common challenges and concerns in treating opioid use disorders, including keeping patients engaged in and completing treatment, managing each patient's risk of relapse and building patients' understanding of relapse and associated coping strategies, dealing with patients leaving treatment early against medical advice, and transitioning patients into the next level of care.

Patient Engagement

Early treatment dropout is a major problem encountered by treatment programs and usually results in poor outcomes for the patient. The phrase "meet patients where they are at" is especially important when treating patients with opioid use disorders. Withdrawal from opioids can be very difficult and can last longer than withdrawal from other substances. Patients in opioid withdrawal may also struggle with impulsivity, limited distress tolerance, poor coping skills, sleep disturbance, and more. It's common for this group of patients to exhibit symptoms and behaviors that complicate treatment. Patients may not show up for scheduled activities or groups and may not respond to change appropriately, or they may have aggressive interpersonal interactions with peers, staff, or family members. The alcohol and drug counselor and multidisciplinary treatment team need to help patients through these issues as well as help them learn better ways to interact with and get support from peers and staff.

Counselors can use motivational enhancement and similar techniques to keep patients engaged in treatment. Counselors can take advantage of the contact patients have with other staff, such as meetings with medical and nursing staff for monitoring withdrawal and providing medications. Use these meetings as times to offer support to patients. If patients feel listened to and supported by staff regarding their difficulties with withdrawal, they will be more open to staff suggestions and encouragement to follow their individual treatment plans. This includes, but is not limited to, getting up, showing up, connecting with their peers, and attending scheduled activities. Engagement of patients in treatment for opioids also includes addressing issues linked to the stages of precontemplation and contemplation.

Consistent use of stage-appropriate motivational enhancement strategies that support motivation, hope, and resiliency is important. Surrounding patients with visual reminders of hope and recovery, offering ongoing education about opioid-specific recovery, supplying increased peer and staff support, and engaging them in wellness activities will help enhance coping skills for cravings and address the sleep issues and chronic pain issues that are frequent symptoms for patients in opioid recovery.

All patients with opioid use disorders—even those who do not engage in MAT—can benefit from attending an opioid-specific support group. If you have access to this type of group, or are able to create a group within your treatment organization, connect patients to the group as soon as possible, ideally during the first week of treatment. As discussed in the previous section, participation in an opioid-specific support group during treatment has been shown to be a critical factor in maintaining long-term recovery.

Risk of Relapse

It is helpful to understand relapse as a predictable and not uncommon symptom of a chronic disease (opioid use disorder) rather than a failure or reason to lose hope that the patient can achieve lasting recovery. During treatment, especially outpatient treatment, some patients may relapse. If opioid-recovery patients relapse while using MAT, the prescribing physician should evaluate the medications and determine whether an adjustment is warranted. It is imperative that the medications not be used as a tool to change behavior. Patients do not benefit from punitive actions, especially those regarding medications.

Patients who demonstrate a pattern of relapse will need to meet with their treatment team to develop a plan for ongoing engagement. This is a time for the patient, any third-party support persons, and the treatment team to discuss the presenting problems, identify recovery risks, and collaborate on the best engagement and risk-reduction strategies.

After any relapse event the counselor should:

• Evaluate the patient's current condition across all ASAM criteria dimensions.

• Assess factors and events prior to the patient's use as well as the use history and related complications during the relapse. (Was the patient invested in the treatment plan? Was the patient taking medications as prescribed? Does the patient need a higher dose of the medication to suppress cravings?)

• Consult with third-party supports as releases allow.

• Assess whether the current medication pathway remains appropriate with modifications or whether a different pathway would be more appropriate.

• Consider what other adjustments are required—for example, an increase in the frequency and type of services, the level of care, or monitoring.

Patients need to know that it is not only important but also essential to be honest with their counselor and to disclose if they have relapsed. In outpatient treatment at the Hazelden Betty Ford Foundation, for example, relapse is not considered a reason for discharge. It is, however, automatically a reason to call a staff meeting to determine the best way to support this patient.

At the Hazelden Betty Ford Foundation, we have found that patients typically fall into the following three tiers with regard to relapse:

• **Level 1 patients** are in significant crisis. They've relapsed or are at risk for an against-staff-advice (ASA) discharge. There are a number of things that can be done to support their re-engagement in the process. For example, consider increasing individual counseling sessions with their alcohol and drug counselor, increasing Twelve Step support group attendance, doing an assignment with their opioid treatment peers on what led up to the relapse, increasing drug testing, or reassessing level of care. For those patients in a treatment program who have chosen not to use medications and are returning to use, it may also be important to revisit their medication decision to determine if a medication path would help.

- **Level 2 patients** have not relapsed but are showing a pattern of warning signs that their engagement is slipping. Examples of such patterns are missing appointments with their alcohol and drug counselor or skipping support group meetings. Counselors will want to have an open, honest discussion with these patients to review those patterns as potential warning signs for relapse.

- **Level 3 patients** are, for all intents and purposes, doing well. Even so, it is helpful to make sure they know there are "normal" difficulties in recovering from an opioid use disorder. Clinicians should also work on helping patients to increase their sense of confidence and resiliency to work through the tough times.

Patients Leaving Treatment against Medical Advice

All atypical discharges present high risks. If you believe a patient is planning to leave treatment against medical advice, pull out all of the "stops," including third-party supports, to interrupt an atypical discharge. Always assess patients for risk of overdose, self-harm, or harm to others, and for medical and mental health complications. Based on this assessment, a seventy-two-hour hold and hospitalization may be needed. Even if criteria for hospitalization are not present, the provider should meet with patients and family members to discuss discharge risks (and provide a document detailing the risks) and make appointments for ongoing services that the patient is willing to accept. Patients should be warned about the risk of overdose if they go back to using opioids after a period of abstinence. Their tolerance may be very low, and using in amounts that they were using prior to treatment may be lethal.

If a patient chooses to discontinue treatment and refuse all services, the provider should emphasize the risks that accompany this decision and encourage the patient to return for services if he or she changes his or her mind in the future and decides to accept help. A follow-up phone call within twenty-four hours from a recovery coach, peer support staff member, or other clinician may lead to re-engaging the patient.

Some patients who leave treatment atypically will opt to return in the future and will repeat the preadmission, triage, and assessment process and undergo an evaluation for a medication pathway to support treatment.

Transitioning to the Next Level of Care

Note that the transfer of a patient to the next level of care, particularly a patient with complex needs related to social stressors, is a dangerous time. Transfers are fraught with patient disappearance, relapse, and risk of overdose due to loss of opioid tolerance. Use "assertive" transfers to ensure that patients actually make it to the next level of care. An assertive transfer is when the treatment clinical staff actively work with the patient and the staff from the next phase of treatment to ensure a smooth transition.

When planning patient discharge with a patient who is using medication-assisted treatment, the treatment team should make sure the patient has continuing access to physicians who can administer medications and should help the patient find community support, such as Twelve Step groups, that is receptive to MAT.

Some treatment programs may help a patient transition to a halfway house or sober living program that helps the person in recovery gradually reintegrate into society. A high percentage of patients with an opioid use disorder require a well-structured and supportive sober living environment outside of their home, in part because many times families, spouses, or partners have set a self-care boundary and will not let the patient return home right away, and in part because the patient needs this type of living environment to support engagement in Twelve Step recovery meetings and the recovery community.

You can find more information on transitioning to the next level of care in Chapter 9: Continuing Care Planning.

7

Medications Used to Treat Opioid Use Disorder

Medication-assisted treatment (MAT) is the use of prescribed medications in combination with an array of other evidence-based interventions or therapies to promote long-term recovery from opioid use disorders. MAT for opioid use disorders includes the use of the following medications: buprenorphine, naltrexone, or methadone. In some programs, only buprenorphine and naltrexone are used. When used under closely supervised care, these medications can reduce cravings for opioids, boost engagement and retention in treatment, and improve the likelihood of achieving long-term abstinence from opioids. This chapter covers medication types, uses, and supporting evidence for medications currently used during the treatment of an opioid use disorder.

Naltrexone

Naltrexone is an *opioid antagonist,* meaning it reduces cravings for opioids by blocking the effects of the drug. It prevents opioids from binding to opioid receptors in the brain so the user doesn't get high. Naltrexone is nonaddictive. It also has no street value.

Naltrexone was approved by the U.S. Food and Drug Administration (FDA) for treatment of opioid use disorders in 1984; its extended-release injectable form was approved in 2010. Extended-release naltrexone is delivered by injection once every twenty-eight days—a feature that can improve medication compliance and overall treatment participation. Extended-release naltrexone injection offers several advantages over the oral form. Though fairly expensive, naltrexone injections are covered by most health insurance plans as a medical procedure. This medication is well tolerated, with mild side effects that can include pain at the injection site, symptoms of the common cold, nausea, insomnia, toothache, and liver enzyme abnormalities.

Naltrexone is also available in an oral form, though compliance with this form of the medication has been shown to be poor.

Keep in mind that naltrexone works only on opioid receptors; therefore, those using it can get intoxicated from alcohol or other drugs—but not from opioids.

Duplicating this page is illegal. Do not duplicate without the publisher's written permission.

55

Patients may try getting intoxicated in this way or by using opioids later in the nal-trexone cycle, when the effects of the drug are wearing off. This can lead to relapse, overdose, and even death if large quantities of other drugs are taken.

While a person is on naltrexone, prescribed opioids for pain will be blocked as well. In emergencies where medications are needed for the treatment of pain (for example, in surgery), the effects of naltrexone can be overcome with a regional anes-thetic or high doses of opioids. This should be done only in a medical setting.

As just mentioned, overdoses are possible during use of extended-release naltrex-one. People sometimes experiment with using opioids to see if naltrexone really does block their effects, or they try to override the opioid blockade in an attempt to get intoxicated. This is extremely dangerous, as there is very little room for error, and overdose is a likely outcome. Close monitoring of patients is needed. Overdoses are associated with all treatments of opioid use disorders, and the data do not yet dis-cern which methods are most likely to prevent this.

Extended-release naltrexone can be provided only after the patient has been free of opioids for seven to ten days. Providing the medication before this time period will result in sudden, extreme opioid withdrawal symptoms. Waiting this long can be very difficult for some patients, especially in an outpatient setting. It's important for patients and their family members to have clear information on the potential prob-lems associated with the use of extended-release naltrexone before making the deci-sion to use this drug.

Research reveals that naltrexone reduces cravings for opioids, prevents relapse, helps people stay in treatment for opioid use disorders, and assists them in following their treatment plan. Extended-release injectable naltrexone has outperformed oral naltrexone in producing these positive outcomes.[1]

Buprenorphine

Buprenorphine was approved by the FDA in 2002 for treatment of opioid use disor-ders. This medication is available as either buprenorphine only or buprenorphine plus naloxone. At the time of this printing, the Hazelden Betty Ford Foundation uses Suboxone, a combination of buprenorphine and naloxone.

Buprenorphine is a *partial opioid agonist,* meaning it activates opioid receptors, just as morphine, heroin, oxycodone, and other opioids do. Users can get high on the medication, but not to the same degree as with other opioids. They experience a "ceil-ing" or threshold effect: above a certain level, buprenorphine fails to increase intox-ication. This effect also applies to respiratory depression, making the medication safer than most other opioids, because people are highly unlikely to overdose. At the same time, buprenorphine has a strong tendency to bind with opioid receptors and so prevents the effects of other opioids.

The side effects of buprenorphine can include nausea, vomiting, dizziness, sweating, hypotension, and miosis (pinpoint pupils). Accidental overdose from buprenorphine use is rare, almost always occurring in combination with other sedative drugs or alcohol.

Buprenorphine has been shown to decrease craving, increase treatment retention, and decrease relapse. Since it is provided by a prescription that patients can take with them, it is much more convenient for patients than methadone, which requires daily attendance at a specially licensed methadone clinic.

For some patients, buprenorphine may have been their first opioid "street drug." It can be diverted and misused: people on buprenorphine can save the medication and sell what they don't use. For these reasons, monitoring and oversight are crucial. In addition, its accessibility via prescription means that buprenorphine can be taken without the supporting treatment structure of regular contact with a therapist and other clinical services, although this is not advised.

The primary reason people misuse buprenorphine is to prevent opioid withdrawal symptoms rather than engage in active addiction. Yet people who misuse the drug find that tolerance develops quickly, and buprenorphine's ceiling effect limits its street value.

Because users can achieve some level of "high" from buprenorphine, its compatibility with an abstinence-based model of treatment and recovery has been controversial. To resolve this issue, it can be helpful to turn to Tradition Three of Alcoholics Anonymous (AA): "The only requirement for A.A. membership is a desire to stop drinking" and Narcotics Anonymous (NA), "The only requirement for N.A. membership is a desire to stop using." The author of *Twelve Steps and Twelve Traditions* notes that this stance evolved only after "years of harrowing experience":

> At last experience taught us that to take away any alcoholic's full chance was sometimes to pronounce his death sentence, and often to condemn him to endless misery. Who dared to be judge, jury, and executioner of his own sick brother?[2]

Suboxone Film is a prescription medicine that contains the active ingredients buprenorphine and naloxone. The naloxone is included to help prevent misuse. If a person is dependent on a full opioid agonist and attempts to inject Suboxone Film, the naloxone will likely cause withdrawal symptoms. It was formulated this way to prevent illicit use for intoxication by intravenous injection.

Studies examining buprenorphine for the treatment of opioid use disorders are positive overall for both youth and adults. Buprenorphine inhibits cravings, reduces relapse, improves treatment retention, and boosts attendance in support groups. Note: to be effective, buprenorphine must be given at a sufficient dose. Treatment providers who give an insufficient dose for a short treatment duration may mistakenly conclude that the medication is ineffective, when in truth the proper dose was not administered.[3]

Methadone

Methadone is an *opioid agonist*. Since the 1960s, it has been the most widely used medication for opioid use disorders. Methadone is available only at licensed clinics—ideally, along with access to other clinical services.

In the context of treatment for opioid use disorders, methadone offers some advantages. When taken daily, it can reduce cravings, decrease withdrawal symptoms, promote abstinence from other opioids, and help people remain functional in daily life. Methadone can meet the needs of certain systems and the audiences that they serve.

However, methadone use also introduces some risks. Because methadone is a full opioid agonist, it is possible for users to get intoxicated. Methadone has considerable street value along with a history of being diverted for nonprescription use. A review of methadone-based treatment (methadone plus psychosocial treatment) found that methadone treatment was effective in reducing opioid use, opioid use-associated transmission of infectious disease, and crime.[4]

■ ■ ■

8

MAT as an Integrated Evidence-Based Practice

This chapter covers medication-assisted treatment (MAT) as an integrated evidence-based practice. This includes research supporting medication use, using medications in conjunction with other evidence-based practices in treatment, comparing MAT to established chronic disease models, engaging family members to support MAT, considerations before starting MAT, and discontinuing MAT with any patient. While many studies show the lifesaving value of MAT for patients with opioid use disorders, MAT medications are not appropriate for all patients.

The Hazelden Betty Ford Foundation COR-12 Program

In 2012, the Hazelden Betty Ford Foundation acknowledged an urgent need to do more for patients with opioid addiction. These patients had often attended treatment several times in the past, had a large degree of clinical severity in addition to their opioid use, and were leaving treatment prematurely. Most critically, some of these patients were overdosing and dying. In response to this, and based on a strong belief that anti-addiction medications have a place in abstinence-based treatment, a cross-disciplinary team of Hazelden Betty Ford Foundation staff designed and implemented an MAT model for patients with opioid use disorder. The core elements of this model, called Comprehensive Opioid Response with the Twelve Steps (COR-12), are (1) the use of buprenorphine/naloxone or naltrexone (where appropriate); (2) Twelve Step–based treatment; (3) individual and group counseling sessions; and (4) the use of evidence-based practices in counseling sessions, such as motivational interviewing (MI) and cognitive-behavioral therapy (CBT).

A core part of the COR-12 program is the use of opioid support groups both during and after treatment. These groups focus on issues and challenges specific to recovering from opioid use disorders, including experiences related to taking medications such as buprenorphine, buprenorphine/naloxone, or naltrexone as part of treatment and recovery.

Duplicating this page is illegal. Do not duplicate without the publisher's written permission.

59

Recovery from any substance use disorder is a long-term process, and the basis of the Hazelden Betty Ford Foundation's COR-12 model is to help patients achieve recovery from opioid use disorder with all of the means available to effectively treat the disorder. The use of medications, both during treatment and as a way to support long-term recovery, is a key component of this approach. The Foundation views patients who take buprenorphine in this way as being abstinent and in recovery, just as patients in recovery from another substance use disorder would be considered in recovery if they were taking prescription opioids as prescribed by their doctor to treat pain after a major surgery. Each patient's recovery trajectory will be different, and some patients may need to take a medication such as buprenorphine over an extended period of time. The overall goal is to get the patient well and on a path to long-term recovery with any clinical means that are beneficial for that patient.

Research Supporting Medication-Assisted Treatment

Many studies have shown that medications such as methadone, buprenorphine, and naltrexone all reduce opioid use and related patient symptoms, and they reduce the risk of infectious disease transmission as well as the criminal behavior associated with drug use.[1] These medications have also been shown to increase treatment retention—and when patients stay in treatment, they have lower rates of death from overdose, reduced risk of HIV and hepatitis C transmission, reduced rates of criminal involvement, and increased rates of employment.[2]

The use of MAT for opioid use disorders is backed by scientific research and is recommended by these organizations:

- Substance Abuse and Mental Health Services Administration (SAMHSA, part of the U.S. Department of Health and Human Services)
- U.S. Veterans Administration
- National Institute on Drug Abuse (NIDA)
- American Society of Addiction Medicine (ASAM)
- Washington Circle—a policy group devoted to improving treatment for substance use disorders

MAT in Conjunction with Other Evidence-Based Practices

While MAT medications are very helpful in the treatment of opioid use disorders, they are not intended to be the primary or only intervention. To promote the greatest success for the patient, these medications are best used in conjunction with other evidence-based practices such as (1) motivational enhancement therapy, (2) psycho-education, (3) cognitive-behavioral interventions, and (4) community-integration interventions.[3] Some programs also include Twelve Step Facilitation (TSF) as one of these core evidence-based approaches.

In this way, medications serve an *adjunctive* role, meaning they are one element in a robust, abstinence-based model of substance use disorder treatment that ideally includes the following:

- inpatient/residential treatment
- intensive outpatient treatment with a step-down to less intensive continuing care
- individual therapy
- group therapy
- active involvement in a community support group (such as a Twelve Step fellowship)
- active involvement of family members/family counseling
- a multidisciplinary treatment team
- physical medical services, if needed
- mental health services, if needed
- sober recovery housing or collegiate recovery housing, if needed
- vocational services, if needed

More details about the psychosocial evidence-based practices used to treat substance use disorders are found in Chapter 6: Effective Treatment of Opioid Use Disorder.

Comparing MAT for Opioids to Other Chronic Disease Models

Using MAT for opioid use disorder is grounded in the following principles, which are widely accepted by researchers and clinicians in the treatment of other chronic diseases, such as asthma or diabetes.

Opioids can profoundly disrupt the reward system in the human brain. This can make recovery from an opioid use disorder very challenging. People with opioid use disorders often have significant difficulties with cravings and withdrawal symptoms and find it hard to stay in treatment long enough to achieve long-term recovery. Also, they often require a much longer period of time to establish abstinence-based recovery as compared to people with other substance use disorders. Medication is helpful in addressing both issues.

Current treatment of asthma, hypertension, diabetes, and other chronic illnesses hinges on the combination of medication with a variety of other clinical interventions. Medication is not pitted against other interventions as an "either-or" proposition; rather, a "both-and" approach is used. Opioid use disorders can be addressed with the same philosophy. With MAT, there is a full spectrum of possibilities for patients, who can benefit from medication at various points during the entire course of their recovery.

We can also learn from the approach of Twelve Step fellowships such as Overeaters Anonymous (OA) and Sex Addicts Anonymous (SAA). Members of these groups do not aim to stop eating or having sex. Rather, they make a clear distinction between behaviors that fuel their disorder and behaviors that support their lifelong recovery. People with opioid use disorders who take buprenorphine or naltrexone are temporarily adopting the same approach by using medications to support recovery until they can safely achieve abstinence.

Engaging Family Members to Support Medication Use

Using MAT for opioid use disorders requires communicating with family members in a different way than with other treatment approaches. Most treatment programs teach family members the Al-Anon approach of detachment with love and letting go. When treating opioid use disorders, the message to family members is very different. Treatment providers need to reach out to family members from the very beginning. During preadmission screening, the family receives information about MAT right along with the patient. Ideally, decisions about whether to enter this form of treatment are made jointly. At this time, it is useful for family members to express any reservations about a loved one's taking "another drug." Providers can explain how medication fits within the full continuum of treatment services, the efficacy of the medications, and how medication use is supervised. It's important for family members to also leverage their influence in keeping the patient engaged in treatment, including using medications as prescribed.

MAT, Abstinence, and Twelve Step Groups

Are people really "drug free" if they take a medication? Aren't they just substituting one drug for another? It's understandable that people would ask this question. They might meet others who attend Twelve Step fellowships, such as AA and NA, who believe that taking medication for a mental health problem—including a problem with opioid use—is a sign of weakness, laziness, or lack of moral character. This belief has been around for decades.

The reality is that while some people choose to use alcohol or illegal drugs, nobody chooses to have a substance use disorder. Alcoholism and other substance use disorders are diseases that wreak havoc in the parts of the brain involved in making choices and controlling behavior. There's no weakness, laziness, or lack of moral character involved when your mind and body tell you that taking a drug is as urgent as taking your next breath. Drugs are what people use to get high. Medications are what people take to get well under a physician's care. Because they will not feel or act high on appropriate doses, people who take medications are not compromising their sobriety.

People who are committed to treatment and recovery learn that there are many differences between substances used to get high and medications used for health. The following chart lists examples of these differences.

TABLE 2

Drug versus Medication[4]

Drug	Medication
The motivation to use a drug is a brain reward (euphoria, getting high).	The motivation to use medication is to prevent and treat an illness.
The pattern of using drugs is marked by dosages and methods of administration—such as injection or smoking—that create spikes and troughs in drug concentration in the blood. The dosage escalates, and the drug is administered more frequently.	The pattern of using medication is marked by dosages, dosing schedules, and methods of administration that produce steady drug concentrations in the blood.
Drug use is characterized by self-monitoring, a progressive loss of control, and secrecy and dishonesty.	Control and monitoring of medication are maintained via open, honest communication with physicians and family members.
The net effect of drug use is a progressive deterioration in the quality of life.	The net effect of medication use is a progressive improvement in the quality of life.
Drug use (other than alcohol use by adults) often involves breaches of the law.	Medication is taken within laws that govern its manufacture, sale, possession, and use.
Drug use is often nested within other self-destructive and socially harmful behaviors.	Medication use is often nested within other health-promoting and recovery-enhancing behaviors.
Drug use is often nested within a drug-saturated social network.	Medication use is nested within a pro-recovery social network.

All patients with opioid use disorders can benefit from attending an opioid-specific support group for social support during and after treatment. These are facilitated meetings where patients with opioid use disorder can share their unique challenges

Duplicating this page is illegal. Do not duplicate without the publisher's written permission.

63

and successes. If you can, start this type of group for your patients as soon as possible, and have them start attending in the first week of treatment. Participation in opioid-specific support groups during inpatient treatment and throughout outpatient treatment into long-term recovery has been proven to be a critical factor in maintaining abstinence for the long term.

Evaluating the Use of MAT for a Particular Patient

MAT should be an *option* for everyone with an opioid use disorder. However, it is not necessarily the "right" path for everyone. People enter treatment with different personal histories and needs. And the elements of effective recovery for any individual can change over time.

A physician who specializes in recovery from opioid use disorders should work with the patient and the treatment team to make a decision about the best treatment option. Here are some factors to consider with MAT:

- the severity and length of the patient's opioid use disorder
- the patient's history of abusing a medication such as buprenorphine
- the patient's history of other sedative misuse
- the patient's recovery history, including how well he or she did in any prior treatment
- the patient's prior experience with MAT
- any contraindications for the patient—conditions such as pregnancy or liver disease that rule out medication as an option
- the patient's mental health history
- the patient's risk for continued opioid use and/or relapse
- the patient's home environment
- the cost of MAT and the patient's financial resources
- the patient's current commitment to treatment and long-term recovery

Considerations in Discontinuing MAT

Any treatment program using MAT should include planning around issues related to discontinuation of medications or crisis situations related to discontinuation of medications. Careful attention to decision making and a discussion on discontinuation are critical, since patients may otherwise leave treatment and stop taking medications on their own, putting themselves at high risk for relapse and overdose.

Providing care from a person-centered perspective is imperative when working with this population. Patients' goals around use of medications will change throughout their recovery process. Some may want to eventually taper off opioid treatment medications, and some continue indefinitely with their medication regimen. The provider should plan for increased contact and support for patients as they transition off medications, as this can be a high-risk period for relapse.

At the Hazelden Betty Ford Foundation, we have observed that abrupt discontinuation of MAT, without discussion and approval by the treatment team, puts the patient at a very high risk for relapse. It is critical for the interdisciplinary treatment team to "be on the same page" when it comes to discontinuation of a medication.

While there is still not enough evidence to indicate an optimal length of medication treatment, at least twelve to eighteen months of stability on medications increases chances at overall recovery. The focus should remain on recovery. Too often, treatment success is defined as the presence or absence of chemical use rather than specific recovery milestones. One set of such milestones is the four major dimensions of recovery published by SAMHSA:[5]

- **Health**—overcoming or managing one's disease(s) or symptoms—for example, abstaining from the use of alcohol, illicit drugs, and nonprescribed medications if one has a substance use disorder—and, for everyone in recovery, making informed, healthy choices that support physical and emotional well-being
- **Home**—having a stable and safe place to live
- **Purpose**—conducting meaningful daily activities, such as a job, school, volunteerism, family caretaking, or creative endeavors, and the independence, income, and resources to participate in society
- **Community**—having relationships and social networks that provide support, friendship, love, and hope

While abstinence is a goal for many people in recovery from opioid use disorder, it is important to respect the individual trajectories of patients on their journey. It's important that patients make an informed choice about whether and when it's appropriate to taper off medications. The decision on when to stop medications during outpatient treatment is best made by the patient in conjunction with an interdisciplinary treatment team: case managers, the alcohol and drug counselor, mental health professionals, and physicians. Input from family members, as well as other identified support persons and third parties, is important.

Finding a Physician and Other Providers

Many patients, upon leaving treatment, will need to find a primary care physician or other primary care provider who understands addiction, especially opioid use disorder and the medications often used in treatment. This is best done before an urgent health problem arises.

You can be of help to patients by compiling a list of local mental health practitioners, primary care physicians, and psychiatrists who provide MAT for opioid use disorders and who understand the use of naltrexone and buprenorphine/naloxone for this purpose. Look for physicians who are certified by the American Board of Addiction Medicine (ABAM) or the American Association of Addiction Psychiatrists (AAAP).

As patients transition back to a home environment, those who remain on naltrexone or buprenorphine/naloxone will need to find a local physician who is authorized to prescribe these medications.

■ ■ ■

9

Continuing Care Planning

The treatment of most chronic conditions (asthma, hypertension, and others) is not considered effective without continuing care by a health care professional.[1] The chronic nature of addiction also requires continuing care to ensure that people are supported throughout the duration of their recovery, especially during the critical period immediately following discharge from an intensive treatment program.

After people leave treatment and go back to their home environment, they often face a range of issues that can include relationship conflicts, legal problems, money worries, medical and mental health challenges, employment hurdles, custody matters, loss of a professional license, re-enrolling at a college or university to complete higher education, and more. People in early recovery from opioid use disorders can benefit from continuing care services as a structured source of extended external support and accountability that goes beyond the initial treatment episode.

Defining *Continuing Care*

Continuing care—also known as aftercare, stepped-down care, extended intervention, or recovery management services—can last for several months following completion of a more intensive treatment program. Continuing care services have been shown to have a significant positive impact on abstinence rates and quality of life after acute treatment for a substance use disorder.[2]

Through the years, the term *continuing care* has been defined many ways. The models of continuing care that have been the most prevalent are peer support groups, such as Alcoholics Anonymous (AA) or Narcotics Anonymous (NA). In some of the research literature, *continuing care* is defined as extended care or any care that includes a step down in care, such as stepping down to outpatient care, entering sober housing, or pairing with a recovery coach following intensive outpatient services.

For most, continuing care planning means providing a means of extended patient monitoring and/or support as a step down after treatment. Regardless of whether

Duplicating this page is illegal. Do not duplicate without the publisher's written permission.

67

the continuing care services involve telephone calls, video chat, text messages with coaches, computer-based programs of engagement, or peer support meetings, the key issue is the need for treatment systems to be accountable for some form of appropriate stepped-down care following an acute episode and treatment completion. Other chronic diseases, such as diabetes, have long used a continuing care approach. As substance use disorders are also chronic diseases requiring long-term management, this approach is increasingly understood and acknowledged in the addiction treatment field.

Recovery Management

William L. White, senior research consultant at Chestnut Health Systems and Lighthouse Institute, describes a fundamental shift in the prevailing paradigm for treatment of substance use disorders. He believes that the field is moving from an emphasis on acute intervention to a focus on recovery management, as evidenced by three changes in the continuum of care.

First, treatment providers are placing greater emphasis on enhancing motivation for change *before* admitting people for services. This includes removing environmental obstacles to recovery and determining what recovering people and their families can accomplish outside of formal intervention.

Second, treatment experiences are involving more services from agencies and providers that are based in the recovering person's community rather than inside the walls of a single treatment center.

Third, the aim of treatment is changing from acute stabilization to long-term recovery maintenance. "Rather than cycling individuals through multiple self-contained episodes of acute treatment," White observes, "recovery management provides an expanded array of recovery support services for a much greater length of time but at a much lower level of intensity and cost per service episode."[3]

The recovery management model acknowledges that recovery most often occurs through incremental (often with ebb and flow) progress within five domains: physical, mental, social, cultural, and spiritual. Recovery management services work to move patients toward self-management of the disease of addiction by teaching the self-care skills needed not only to initiate but also to sustain a lifelong substance-free lifestyle and improved quality of life across these five domains of living. This means providing patient education and skills on multiple topics, including relapse prevention, Twelve Step recovery and spiritual health, family and relationships, mental health, emotional health, physical health, employment and vocational skills, and life skills.[4]

Addiction as a Chronic, Relapsing Disease

Although long viewed as a chronic disease, severe and persistent alcohol and other substance use disorders have historically been treated as self-contained, acute episodes of care rather than as a long-lasting condition that can be controlled but not cured. The acute model of treatment may be characterized like this: professionals assess and admit a patient to a course of inpatient or outpatient treatment, then discharge that patient to aftercare, and then evaluate whether treatment "worked" by measuring the effect of this single episode of care on the patient's ability to continue to maintain abstinence and psychosocial adjustment as measured over a very brief follow-up period.[5]

Although some patients can be successfully treated within an acute care model, more than half the patients entering publicly funded addiction programs require multiple episodes of treatment over several years to achieve and sustain recovery.[6] Even though we understand the substance use disorder as a chronic, relapsing disease, when patients participate in one treatment episode and then relapse back into alcohol or other drug use, clinicians and others may still depict them as a "treatment failure" rather than acknowledge that substance use disorders often involve recurrent cycles of relapse and recovery. Because a substance use disorder is a chronic, relapsing disease, patients often present with symptoms and severity that ebb and flow over an extended period of time in their lives.

The chronic nature of substance use disorders requires an extended focus on sustaining or improving patient engagement, enhancing each patient's motivation for change, addressing barriers to recovery, creating continuing care programs based on the individual's needs and support network, and, where appropriate, extended periods of patient assessment and monitoring to determine whether the patient and his or her family can sustain recovery without continued professional intervention. In this way, recovery management does not attempt to replace the acute model but instead seeks to wrap that model in a larger continuum of support that expands the focus from treatment of a patient's acute symptoms to help each patient work toward self-sufficiency in maintaining his or her ongoing life in recovery.

Following are key talking points to share with your patients about the need for immediate engagement with continuing care:

- Your time in treatment itself is only the first step in recovery. Experience has shown that simply stopping opioid or other drug use is not enough. This idea is central to Twelve Step recovery. In fact, only Step One of Alcoholics Anonymous is about substance use. The rest of the Steps are about changing your beliefs, changing your behaviors, and developing spiritual practices.

- You will be returning home to a life where substance use may have been a "normal" event. You may be faced with many of the problems you had when you left for treatment—challenges posed by legal, financial, emotional, family, relationship, or employment concerns. Your continuing care plan will help you with this adjustment.

- Research indicates that the period of time immediately after treatment is critical to building lasting sobriety. Consistent and daily support, accountability, and guidance from a "circle of support" (professionals, recovering community, family, and friends) are critical elements in achieving abstinence and a program of lifelong recovery. It is essential that you seek out a supportive community to help you on your journey.

- The bottom line: continuing care is an essential part of lifelong recovery. And the sooner it is started, the more successful you will be. You've overcome your own personal hurdles. We urge you to continue the momentum you've started. Learn from those who have gone before you and follow in the footsteps of their success. Start your continuing care plan now.

Many people being discharged from residential or outpatient treatment programs are referred to some type of continuing care service after completing treatment. In discharge planning, the treatment team should discuss these continuing care options with patients:

1. Transitioning into sober living
2. Utilizing a recovery coach
3. Engaging with community support
4. Engaging with Twelve Step or other peer support meetings

Sober Living Appropriate for MAT

Sober living residences are often recommended for individuals transitioning from inpatient services and/or those who lack strong support outside of treatment—including those whose home and family living situation put their recovery at risk. If you frequently treat patients with opioid use disorders, reach out to local sober living houses and talk with their administrators about referring your patients there who are still on medication-assisted treatment (MAT). Some sober living administrators may have serious concerns about opening their doors to people who take buprenorphine/naloxone, especially if it means having to store the medication on the premises, where it can be diverted. Some sober houses have designed a way to store buprenorphine/naloxone in safes and locked offices, and they arrange for the house manager to observe patients' self-administration of this medication.

Other sober living administrators will allow someone taking buprenorphine/ naloxone to live at the sober house, but they will not keep the medication on site, requiring the medication to be taken at home, with a sponsor, or at the outpatient facility. Outpatient treatment centers should consider the option of holding medications on site for patients to self-administer, as this can reduce the risk of misuse and diversion for patients living in sober housing or at home. Be prepared to explain to your local sober housing staff the rationale for your use of this medication and cite supporting research for the efficacy of medications as part of effective treatment.

Remember that individual sober living houses offer varying levels of therapeutic community over time. During good months, a house will be filled with people who are committed to recovery and serious about working on their program. That can change within a week or two as people exit the house and new residents move in. This is an important variable to monitor with your outpatient patients. During individual and group therapy, encourage them to bring up any issues related to their sober living experience.

Recovery Coaching

Recovery coaching is a form of strengths-based support that helps an individual in early recovery from a substance use disorder. Engagement with a recovery coach may be best initiated as an immediate step down from treatment. Some coaches are licensed addiction treatment counselors, while others may have only coaching licensure. Conversations between the coach and patient are offered with various models, including phone calls, video conferencing, text-based messages, or platform-based private messages.

Some coaching programs leverage technology to aid in patient monitoring with regard to compliance to a treatment plan or patient goals. The highest level of monitoring occurs through technology such as random breathalyzer testing (using a wireless sensor connected to a smartphone), and newer models are emerging using wearable biometric sensors. Other methods of patient monitoring include the use of artificial intelligence such as natural language processing to leverage computers to monitor peer support conversations and notify a coach if the language points to a risk of relapse or suicide.

When a patient steps down from treatment into recovery coaching, communication may begin the first week post-discharge and occur weekly while gradually decreasing in frequency over the duration of the program (often anywhere from six to eighteen months).

Coaching sessions should include ongoing screening of individual needs and intervention for emerging issues, with a solution-focus to address the patient's current commitment to action toward recovery goals. In addition to monitoring the newly recovering individual, the coach may submit monthly verification reports to key stakeholders, including the participant, family, and other contacts, such as the legal system or employer.

An intensive level of recovery coaching as a posttreatment support is ideal for people who need additional encouragement and accountability, such as those facing legal issues, custody matters, or loss of their professional license; people who've been in treatment multiple times; and students who are returning to college.

Community Support

After completing inpatient and outpatient treatment, people in early recovery can stay connected through informal sources of continuing care. Examples include unit reunions, alumni meetings, service opportunities, retreats, workshops, and other special events designed for fun and fellowship. There are often many methods of getting involved, including participating in recovery group discussions, chats, blogs, and online meetings; listening to recovery lectures; watching recovery videos; or joining book club discussions.

Twelve Step or Similar Peer Support

Twelve Step programs are based on a model of peer support or "fellowship" where individuals regularly connect with other people who can understand and identify with the challenges and successes of managing ongoing recovery from a substance use disorder. Twelve Step groups include AA, NA, Cocaine Anonymous (CA), and many others. People who attend peer support groups like AA or NA often utilize a sponsor who can help them work the Twelve Steps, help them see their progress, offer guidance and support, and keep them honest and accountable.

AA is an informal program whose members share a common goal: help each other stay sober. At meetings, the principles behind the Twelve Steps and Twelve Traditions are explored. Members tell their stories, emphasizing how they failed and how they succeeded. They answer the questions of newcomers and help each other stay sober just for today. They listen, and they keep what they hear private.

NA is a nonprofit fellowship whose primary purpose is to help people abstain from using drugs. NA got its start from AA. NA is based on the Twelve Steps and Twelve Traditions of AA. The Twelve Steps of AA/NA have been described as a road map to abstinence—to a life free of drugs and alcohol. NA offers group meetings that put you in touch with those who share your experiences and offers ideas about starting and maintaining a healthy, lifelong recovery.

Despite the trend that MAT (in conjunction with evidence-based recovery programs and Twelve Step approaches) is becoming accepted as a best practice for treating opioid use disorder, stigma surrounding medication use still exists in the Twelve Step recovery community. Some Twelve Step group members may confront patients with strong opinions that using medications means they are not totally abstaining from mood-altering substances. This can be a very shaming, negative experience, especially for a patient in early recovery who has just completed treatment and is practicing recovery support by going to Twelve Step meetings.

Educate patients about the stigma attached to medication that still prevails in some Twelve Step fellowships. Talk with local AA or NA groups, or talk with treatment alumni to identify peer support groups that are accepting of people using MAT and share those recommendations with your patients. Some treatment facilities that have not been able to find MAT-supporting peer support locally have started their own on-site peer recovery meetings for patients in recovery from opioid use disorders where all patients can attend, regardless of whether they are using medication or not.

Organizations such as LifeRing Secular Recovery, SMART Recovery, Double Trouble in Recovery, Women for Sobriety, or Methadone Anonymous are groups that accept members who are taking MAT for opioid use disorder. Many of these groups offer physical peer-to-peer support meetings, and some offer online forums or chat groups. More details about these and other peer support groups are included in Appendix B: Peer Support Resources.

■ ■ ■

Duplicating this page is illegal. Do not duplicate without the publisher's written permission.

73

Part 3

Case Studies

10

Treatment Challenges and Solutions

CASE STUDY 1

Combatting Clinical Nihilism

Expert: Cathy Stone, Manager of the COR-12 Program, St. Paul, Minnesota

---

One big challenge for clinicians treating patients for opioid use disorder is clinical or therapeutic nihilism, or the belief that little can be done for these patients, and how this may limit treatment effectiveness. This is a risk providers face as they work in this new era where opioid addiction has reached epidemic proportions.

There are two primary sources of clinical or therapeutic nihilism:

1. The belief that there is little hope for most of these patients in truly achieving and maintaining recovery. The relapse rate is very high, and death from relapse is even higher as patients who, during treatment, have detoxified from opioids and remained abstinent quickly lose their tolerance to the drug. The patient who suddenly goes back to using opioids in the same amount he or she previously used can easily overdose and experience respiratory depression, which can be fatal.

2. The belief that the clinician can't be effective with these patients. The same strategies and skill-building techniques that work with other substance use patients fail to work with opioid patients. The progress of these patients in treatment can be very slow. They have more difficulty with building relationships, building interpersonal trust, engaging with the Twelve Step community, and developing their own sense of self-efficacy. Their rates of relapse are high. They have more trouble remembering and making it to appointments or complying with similar behavioral requests.

Patient Case: Ben in Outpatient Treatment Is at High Risk of Relapse

Ben is a twenty-nine-year-old male patient who is in outpatient treatment for opioid use disorder. At his last outpatient treatment meeting with his counselor, Ben reported very high cravings and says he hasn't taken his buprenorphine/naloxone for the last few days. It's a Friday, and Ben tells his counselor that he is excited to spend the weekend with his girlfriend, Jessica, whom he hasn't seen for the last month because she's been out of town. This is a potentially risky situation since the clinician knows that Ben and Jessica frequently used drugs together in the past. In this situation, the counselor is extremely concerned about Ben because (1) his drug of choice is opioids, (2) his plan to stay with his girlfriend this weekend puts him at risk, and (3) if he relapses, he is in real danger of overdose and even death. The counselor is truly afraid for Ben and feels a sense of helplessness because she can't control the situation or outcome.

The Challenge for Clinicians

"When a clinician is working with a population of people that is so high-risk for overdose and death, it affects you differently than it would affect you working with a more general population of people," says Cathy Stone, manager of the Comprehensive Opioid Response with the Twelve Steps (COR-12) program in St. Paul, Minnesota. It's easy to feel hopeless and anxious about the day-to-day safety of these patients, and that can negatively affect the way a clinician delivers treatment. If not addressed, this can negatively impact patient care and create higher rates of clinician burnout and turnover. "As a clinician, you can feel pushed back on your heels a bit. You just feel like you're putting out fires, you're not being effective," says Stone. "You have low energy. You feel hopeless for the population you are working with. It's not motivating." It's easy for a provider to start to feel "there's no hope for these people anyway; none of them are ever going to get better. And even if they could, I'm not effective enough to be helpful," Stone says. When all three of these factors occur, you can easily get full-fledged burnout.

In a case like Ben's, "You're likely going to feel anxiety, like you are holding your breath for that patient to make it back to treatment safely on Monday," says Stone. While the concern about relapse is real for all patients in treatment, regardless of their drugs of choice, counselors are especially concerned for patients addicted to opioids because of their high risk of death from respiratory suppression that can occur because the patient's tolerance to opioids falls quickly with abstinence from the drug.

To educate Ben, the clinician will have a conversation with him about the risks of relapse, safety plans, and other supports that he can tap into over the weekend, says Stone. The clinician will make sure Ben understands he is at a greater risk of overdose and death if he relapses because his tolerance is lower since he hasn't been using opioids. These are important practical conversations to have. "As a clinician, you must manage the emotional experience of your own fear for the patient's safety," says Stone. With patients using opioids, this fear is amplified and can affect the counselor's therapeutic approach, causing the counselor to put too much focus on instruction at the expense of listening to the patient and understanding his or her history and motivations. This lack of understanding can reduce the counselor's therapeutic alliance with the patient.

Fearing that Ben may relapse or even overdose on the weekend, the clinician may spend most of the time in their Friday night appointment talking about what Ben should and should not do, without first understanding his feelings and motivations. The counselor might say, "You really shouldn't be spending time with your significant other this weekend. I'm really worried about the fact that you stopped using your medication." The counselor might continue by telling the patient what to do: "I think you should call your sponsor, go to meetings, and tell your sober house about your plan to spend the weekend with your girlfriend." Stone explains that this may culminate with the practitioner telling the patient, "If you spend the weekend with your girlfriend, I'm concerned that you're going to relapse." This may cause Ben to defensively reply, "No, no, no, I'm not going to relapse. I will be fine."

If Ben does relapse over the weekend, he may avoid coming back to treatment on Monday because he doesn't want to face his peers and tell his counselor that he *did* go back to using. In this case, the counselor can best deliver education about the potential for relapse by using motivational enhancement techniques to move Ben toward making smart choices together with the counselor rather than pushing a laundry list of "to-do's" toward Ben.

What You Can Do

How can you practice with this very high-risk population without allowing your emotional experience to interfere with using effective methods to create change?

BUILD A STRONG THERAPEUTIC ALLIANCE

Starting with patient-directed conversation and engaging patients about what they are feeling can establish a foundation of trust. As Stone explains, when the counselor takes the time "to therapeutically put yourself in [your patient's] shoes and understand what that experience might be like," the focus shifts away from the counselor's own emotional response and creates a safe space for the patient to openly discuss his or her experience. Stone suggests asking questions, then listening to and reframing the patient's responses. Using Ben's example, the practitioner could ask how he's feeling about what might happen over the weekend, being mindful that he hasn't seen his significant other for some time. The counselor might say, "Tell me what it's like to think about seeing her again." Ben could then describe what he's excited about, which could be everything from "We just have a lot of fun together" to "I'm excited to have sex." With Ben feeling more comfortable and less judged, the counselor can direct the conversation to any worries Ben may be feeling and ask, "Is there anything you're nervous about?" The door has been opened to talk about potential risks the situation presents—from the patient's point of view.

Within this therapeutic framework, the overly directive expression of concern is replaced with honest discussion. The counselor can use motivational interviewing and phrase questions in an open-ended style that lets the patient explain his or her motivations and goals. Instead of saying, "Don't you think it's a bad idea for you to spend time with your girlfriend?" the practitioner might ask, "Are you worried about the strength of your girlfriend's recovery or any temptations there might be to use together?" This way, if the patient voices concerns, saying something like, "I really hope that wouldn't happen, but I guess it could," the clinician can talk about safety measures without the patient feeling judged. This might lead to a conversation about the importance of naloxone (Narcan) in an overdose situation. They might also talk about supportive people who are familiar with the situation, and how the patient could reach out to these people. Stone explains that even a simple text message can be a reminder that there are people in the patient's corner.

As a counselor, retaining your fidelity to this therapeutic process and working to build a stronger therapeutic alliance will yield valuable insights to support the patient's treatment. The key, Stone says, is "doing the therapeutic work to allow the patient to direct the conversation and using your skills as a clinician to try to understand what motivates the patient." For example, the patient might say, "My girlfriend knows me really well, and I have a really good time with her. I haven't had sex in, like, forever, and I just really want to do that, too." Stone explains how the clinician can reflect back: "You feel safe with her; it's fun and it's exciting. What does it feel like to be excited about something as a sober person?" This may lead to the realization: "This is the first time I've been excited about anything since I got sober." You now have created a foundation where you can talk about managing excitement without chemical use, which is particularly important because boredom and loneliness are considered risk factors for relapse.

Building trust and open, nonjudgmental communication between counselor and patient is an essential part of treatment, helping the patient stay engaged and actively practicing an effective treatment plan in cooperation with treatment staff. "There's a lot of rich conversation that can be had, and it can be so much more effective for the patient to be the one who's helping guide that conversation," Stone says. This also helps patients feel like their counselor wants to understand their process without judging them. The goal is managing the clinician's emotional response to short-term concerns (such as safety) while also creating safety within the therapeutic relationship so the patient continues to share experiences openly. To Stone, this is particularly important, "because if they struggle at all after that experience, I want them to be able to talk to their counselor about it. If they don't struggle, and they find that they want to keep spending time with this person, I want them to talk to their counselor about it."

How can you objectively know whether you have a strong therapeutic alliance with your patient? Try routinely using a short patient assessment, such as the Working Alliance Inventory-Short Revised (WAI-SR), which assesses three key aspects of the therapeutic alliance: (a) agreement on the tasks of therapy, (b) agreement on the goals of therapy, and (c) development of an affective bond. More about the WAI-SR is in Appendix A: Screening, Assessment, and Diagnostic Tools.

■ ■ ▦

Duplicating this page is illegal. Do not duplicate without the publisher's written permission.

81

CASE STUDY 2

Setting Realistic Goals and Expectations

Expert: Cathy Stone, Manager of the COR-12 Program, St. Paul, Minnesota

One common challenge faced by clinicians lies in setting realistic expectations of their patients in treatment for opioid use disorders. When clinicians fail to recognize the differences in how opioid patients progress in treatment compared to those with other types of substance use disorders, their patients can easily feel like failures when they can't reach the unrealistic goals set for them.

Patients who are dependent on opioids face unique challenges that can undermine their ability to remain in treatment and ultimately achieve long-term recovery. They are hypersensitive to physical and psychic pain and are highly vulnerable to stressful events, putting them at greater risk of relapse. They are more likely than other patients to leave treatment before completing it, and they are at higher risk of death from accidental overdose during relapse because of their reduced tolerance levels. Deaths can occur after treatment and during a period of abstinence, when people relapse and return to using the same doses they were taking prior to treatment, for which the body no longer has tolerance, causing respiratory depression.

"Patients in recovery from opioids are different than many other patients we see," says Cathy Stone, manager of the COR-12 program in St. Paul, Minnesota. "The progress of patients in treatment for opioid use disorder can be very slow. The same strategies and skill-building techniques that work with other substance use patients may fail to work on opioid patients." These patients have more difficulty with building relationships, building interpersonal trust, engaging with the Twelve Step community, and developing their own sense of self-efficacy. Their rate of relapse is high. They also have more trouble remembering appointments and complying with other behavioral requests.

Opioid use disorder is complex and frequently requires more interventions, including treatment protocols that incorporate medication-assisted treatment (MAT). The need for medication presents its own set of challenges unique to this patient group, such as difficulty managing medications to control cravings with minimal side effects. Patients in MAT also may face stigma within the Twelve Step community due to the way in which some members define abstinence.

Patient Case: Anton Misses Treatment Appointments and Activities

Anton is twenty-two years old and in the early weeks of treatment for opioid use disorder. He has arrived late or missed most of his appointments in the last week. His clinician needs to be cautious about automatically equating poor behavioral compliance with low motivation. When the topic of a missed appointment comes up, Anton may even acknowledge that he was given reminders and say, "Oh man, I was supposed to go do that urinalysis; you told me to do that, and I just spaced it." As Stone explains, the reality is that maybe Anton is having memory issues, or maybe he has a history of trauma and is anxious about being observed doing a urinalysis, or maybe he just can't stay focused right now. Stone explains that these struggles are common with opioid patients. "This population has a real struggle with executive functioning, and they have a really difficult time with time management and keeping track of things," says Stone. "Sometimes you have to see that 'Hey, this kid is trying, but he can't remember anything right now.'" The important thing is not to make quick assumptions about the patient's motivations and instead to dig deeper to identify what is really going on with the patient.

The Challenge for Clinicians

Clinicians unfamiliar with treating patients with opioid use disorder may set goals similar to those for a patient with alcoholism or cocaine use, and the reality is that recovery for the patient who used opioids will often look very different. There are many factors that contribute to the slower rate of progress for opioid patents, which makes it challenging to provide effective treatment. For instance, opioid use alters the brain and can result in cognitive impairment, which may affect areas like attention and memory, making it harder for these patients to make appointments and manage daily life. These impairments could also dampen their participation in group discussion if patients have difficulty paying attention or remembering what they want to say. These patients are also more sensitive to physical and psychological stress,[1] which could make them want to avoid discussions that they fear will be challenging or uncomfortable.

Remembering to take into account the physical and neural aspects of opioid use can help practitioners understand the challenges facing their patients and see patient behavior from a realistic perspective. This perspective can help practitioners set appropriate goals and inform which strategies they use. It can also help them educate their opioid patients so they understand substance use disorder as a brain disease and not a weakness in their character.[2] While much of the medical community accepts the definition of addiction as "a chronic, relapsing brain disease that is characterized by compulsive drug seeking and use, despite harmful consequences,"[3] some practitioners still have punitive reactions to a patient returning to use.

Setting realistic expectations about the neurobiology of the disease of addiction helps patients see progress and feel successful even if that progress is slow, which is crucial for maintaining their motivation to remain in treatment.

Patients find that appointments with multiple practitioners—doctors, therapists, psychiatrists, and addiction counseling staff—are a lot to manage, especially if those patients have compromised executive function. Stone says it helps to create a treatment program that is fully integrated, with fewer external appointments to remember and manage.

What You Can Do

Having appropriate expectations, rooted in a strong understanding of opioid addiction and the particular challenges it presents, is key to maintaining a healthy perspective about patient progress. It's also important to remember that each patient is unique, and outcomes in treating opioid use disorder will vary, just as they will with any other condition, such as heart disease or stroke.[4] With this in mind, set realistic, achievable goals for patients.

Once realistic goals have been set, be willing to spend more time and effort to support patients in reaching them. For instance, these patients may need reminders of appointments. Additionally, you may need to take time to consider what could be contributing to their behavior and adjust treatment strategies accordingly. For instance, if a patient's participation in group discussion looks different than it does with other types of patients, you may want to consider their vulnerability to stress or possible attention issues.

ADJUST YOUR EXPECTATIONS AND SET REALISTIC PATIENT GOALS

Stone is an advocate for focusing on what the patient needs and being realistic about what he or she is capable of doing. Patients like Anton "may not have the same cognitive ability as typical patients at that point in treatment," she says. Stone explains that clinicians need to ask, "How is [opioid use disorder] manifesting in this person? What are the things that need to happen for this person to have a life that's happy and healthy and free of chemicals? And what can I do to help the patient take the steps they need to get further down the road?"

Understanding what these patients need may also require looking more deeply at what the patient is actually capable of doing at any given time. For example, when Anton misses yet another appointment, his clinician may assume the need to address motivation, but there may be a deeper need than that. As Stone says, "You realize they can't do it. It's not about want, it's about ability." The patient in this example may need an escort to get to meetings or a setting that allows for care to be delivered in one place. You may need to structure a program so that there are fewer "moving parts," reducing the need for patients like Anton to juggle multiple appointments in various locations. "Instead of having unrealistic expectations, we need to create a supportive environment by anticipating and offering accommodations to help with these cognitive needs," Stone says.

With patients who have such extensive needs, there are always limitations to what clinicians are able to do. "You will do what you can, but that may not be enough," Stone explains. Accepting that as a reality of the situation, rather than a personal or professional shortcoming, is important. "And that way," Stone says, "you're able to celebrate the small wins that you see and have an appropriate sense of influence in the change process." This, in turn, supports patients in celebrating their wins, too. When a goal is too high, such as "complete treatment," it is nearly impossible to measure progress. A smaller goal with a short timeline, such as "I will make it to all five of my appointments this week," gives patients something concrete to focus on over the course of a few days and allows them the chance to feel success sooner.

To measure whether the practitioner has been effective requires looking at the patient's situation in its entirety. To illustrate this, Stone offers the story of a friend who works for a facility that treats patients with severe mental health disorders. A typical patient there may be homeless, have a poorly managed mental health disorder, have trouble with medication compliance, may not have any social support from family or friends, and may not be able to hold a job. In this example, if progress is only defined by having every single one of these problems solved, the care provider will feel discouraged most of the time. Also, the patient may feel like a hopeless failure and stop coming for care.

"The population of people with opioid use disorder is similar—we need to focus on and celebrate the small wins," says Stone. When practitioners are able to redefine progress for these patients, within the full context of the unique challenges facing them, they can be rewarded with seeing how significant each step in their patient's treatment is—no matter how small it may first appear. As Stone's friend explains, "This work can take years, and the progress can be very slow. I have to understand what small progress looks like and how to celebrate it. Because when I can do that, then I see wins all over the place."

■   ■   ■

Duplicating this page is illegal. Do not duplicate without the publisher's written permission.

85

CASE STUDY 3

Addressing Trauma

Expert: Cathy Stone, Manager of the COR-12 Program, St. Paul, Minnesota

Addressing trauma is a fundamentally important yet challenging issue in treating patients recovering from opioid use disorder. Clinicians must understand how the past trauma patients may have experienced is impacting them now. Opioid users are more likely to have experienced trauma than patients in treatment for other types of substance use, and there is a direct connection between the emotional pain trauma causes and the analgesic, numbing qualities of opioids. Because trauma undermines a person's ability to feel safe or to trust others (including themselves), establishing a safe therapeutic environment is crucial.

People who suffer trauma are at greater risk for a host of behavioral problems and mental health disorders. Of particular concern are adverse childhood experiences (ACEs), which can disrupt a child's neurodevelopment, resulting in impaired cognitive functioning or the reduced ability to cope with negative emotions. This can lead to developing unhealthy coping mechanisms such as self-harm or substance use. Examples of ACEs include

- physical, sexual, or emotional abuse
- physical or emotional neglect
- witnessing or being the victim of domestic abuse
- mental illness and/or substance misuse within the household
- parental separation or divorce
- having a parent or household member incarcerated

Research has shown that the link between ACEs and later behavioral problems is stronger depending on the number of ACEs reported and the age when the earliest experience happened. For example, having any ACEs increased the risk of a suicide attempt twofold to fivefold, according to a 2001 study.[5] A 2017 study found that individuals reporting six or more ACEs had 24.6 times the odds of attempting suicide.[6] The link between ACEs and prescription drug use was even greater: with each ACE reported, the rate of nonmedical prescription drug use increased by 62 percent, according to a 2017 study on ACEs and adolescent prescription drug use.[7]

The link between opioid use and ACEs is remarkably strong. For instance, one sample of opioid-dependent outpatients seeking buprenorphine treatment showed the vast majority (80.5 percent) reported childhood trauma. A study comparing opioid users to cocaine users found opioid users were more likely to have experienced childhood trauma (90.2 percent versus 60.0 percent) and at a younger age. In addition to being more likely to have experienced childhood trauma, and at a younger age, 90 percent of the opioid users studied reported more than one ACE.[8]

Suffering trauma profoundly impacts the way people experience the world, and relationships in particular, because people experiencing trauma learn to think that others are not necessarily trustworthy. They learn that even people they love may abandon or harm them. Not only does this undermine trauma victims' ability to trust other people, but it undermines their own self-image. As Stone explains, "With that experience of hurt is also a message that there's something wrong with them. They are to blame, and they are not to trust themselves."

As the research described above shows, there is a strong relationship between childhood trauma and opioid use. That trauma needs to be addressed in treatment, or the same issues will continue to undermine a person's recovery. Fortunately, through awareness and use of strategies to address trauma alongside substance use, clinicians can effectively support patients to develop healthy coping strategies and a better quality of life.

Patient Case: Mary Suffers from Trauma

Trauma's far-reaching impact—and close association with opioid use—is apparent in patients such as Mary, a twenty-six-year-old woman in treatment for opioid use disorder. In early conversations with her counselor, it became clear that relational trauma has played a big part in Mary's struggles, and she eventually shared that she was the victim of sexual abuse by a family member as a young child. This experience has left Mary with the inability to form healthy boundaries in her relationships. Childhood abuse often sets up a dangerous pattern, which can make it more likely for victims to end up in abusive relationships as adults or even find themselves in prostitution. As Stone explains, a child in an abusive situation may either have boundaries that are too distant, keeping everyone far away, or boundaries that are too close, essentially leaving no boundaries at all between them and those around them. Stone says: "As a kid, [in order to] reconcile how emotionally hard all of that is and the fact that you have to be okay with this physical boundary being different than the way it should be as a child, you might put up walls completely, or

Duplicating this page is illegal. Do not duplicate without the publisher's written permission.

87

you might lose your physical boundaries altogether, acting as if 'nothing bothers me' when in reality you feel unsafe."

The Challenge for Clinicians

The challenge for clinicians is to understand and address relational trauma as part of treatment for opioid use disorders. This includes understanding the specific connection between trauma and patients using opioids as their drug of choice in their attempt to numb or escape the unpleasant feelings related to their trauma. As Stone explains, "These patients had to learn to cope. They are literally doing the best they can, but the reality is that their experience of the world is painful, and the drugs help them feel normal—to not feel that sort of pain." For patients whose psychological development may have been negatively impacted by traumatic experiences, this may ring especially true as their ability to develop healthy ways of coping or of staying safe may have been stunted.

The experience of trauma and opioid use leaves many patients without a strong sense of self. To cope with their fears of betrayal, abandonment, or being negatively judged, they may be extremely hesitant to share what they are feeling and experiencing. As Stone explains, this makes treating these patients difficult: "When they sit in your office, they don't want to talk to you about stuff. They're not looking forward to opening up. They've got their guard up." What's worse is that opioid patients often feel more comfortable, even safer, around others who use because they know they won't judge each other about using drugs.

What You Can Do
Counselors can help their patients address relational trauma during treatment by being responsive and by creating a safe environment where patients feel like they can be honest and receive nonjudgmental support. To describe her approach, Stone says, "We try to create an environment where [patients] get to struggle, and it's okay for the patient to admit they are struggling. Because if you [a patient] are actually a mess, I'd rather you admit you are a mess than hide it from me." She goes on to say this also applies to the patient being honest about current drug use. "We want to understand it—we want to use it as an opportunity to learn about what was going on that caused it."

Part of establishing a safe and trusting therapeutic environment is accepting that patients are likely to associate you, their current counselor, with any past negative therapeutic experiences they may have had. It is also important to recognize that past experiences with counselors may have resulted in patients feeling shamed, making them even more hesitant to share openly now. "Whether you like it or not, as a counselor, you will represent [to the patient] every other counselor who has ever worked with that person," Stone says. "So if that patient has ever had a counselor who judged them or shamed them or kicked them out of treatment for using or kicked them out of treatment for getting in a relationship with another patient, they're going to assume that you will treat them the same way until you prove to them otherwise."

Patients may also have trouble articulating, or even being able to determine, what they need. As Stone explains, it is up to the counselor to listen carefully. Especially early in treatment, the counselor will need to listen carefully for clues that ACEs or past traumatic experiences are present, even if the patient is not directly disclosing it. For example, a patient may say, "If you felt like me, you would use, too," which Stone explains could be a sign of underlying emotional trauma. "These patients have no idea that trust and safety is what they're needing. Your therapeutic framework must come from the understanding of how trauma affects human beings and that their escapist behavior is purposeful." The counselor's ultimate goal is, of course, to help the patient replace this desire to numb or escape unpleasant feelings with new, healthy coping strategies. But first, the patient must feel safe.

UNDERSTAND THE PRINCIPLES OF A TRAUMA-INFORMED APPROACH

While some opioid patients who have experienced ACEs or trauma as adults will not have a post-traumatic stress disorder (PTSD) diagnosis, treatment that incorporates trauma-informed approaches may be beneficial. As with other co-occurring disorders, it is recommended that patients with the dual diagnosis of substance use disorder and PTSD receive treatment for both at the same time.

According to the Substance Abuse and Mental Health Services Administration (SAMHSA), a trauma-informed treatment approach is different from the type of trauma-specific care delivered by facilities that specialize in trauma. A trauma-informed approach can be implemented in any type of care facility. According to SAMHSA's concept of a trauma-informed approach, "A program, organization, or system that is trauma-informed:

- *Realizes* the widespread impact of trauma and understands potential paths for recovery;
- *Recognizes* the signs and symptoms of trauma in [patients], families, staff, and others involved with the system;
- *Responds* by fully integrating knowledge about trauma into policies, procedures, and practices; and
- Seeks to actively resist *re-traumatization*."[9]

Topics likely to be of special importance to opioid patients with a history of trauma include safety, boundaries, emotional regulation and resilience, and self-care. They may also benefit from a basic understanding about how trauma can impact psychological development and how opening up and discussing their feelings is an important first step in starting to address the shame and self-blame they may be feeling. The good news is that studies have shown that treating trauma and substance use disorder together will benefit recovery from both disorders. It can offer patients relief from the pain and shame they may have carried for years—and hope for a better life.

There are several specialized programs for training clinicians in trauma-specific interventions. Hazelden Publishing offers evidence-based programs by top experts in the field to help both women and men heal from trauma. Visit hazelden.org/bookstore and enter "trauma" in the search field. A list of trauma-specific interventions compiled by SAMHSA can be found at www.samhsa.gov/nctic/trauma-interventions.

■ ■ ■

CASE STUDY 4

Finding an MAT-Supportive Peer Group

Expert: Cathy Stone, Manager of the COR-12 Program, St. Paul, Minnesota

Finding a peer recovery support group, such as Alcoholics Anonymous (AA) or Narcotics Anonymous (NA), that is accepting of the use of medication-assisted treatment (MAT) is a challenge for clinicians and their patients in treatment for opioid use disorder. Even as MAT (in conjunction with evidence-based recovery programs and Twelve Step approaches) is becoming accepted as a best practice for treating opioid use disorder, stigma remains a significant problem because some in the recovery community feel that sobriety has not been achieved if a patient is taking medication.

Members of peer support groups may confront MAT patients with the idea that using medications means they are not "totally abstaining" from mood-altering substances and may view the use of medications as a crutch. They may have negative associations with MAT medications, such as methadone, as substances that are commonly abused by people who use them to get high. Faced with this stigma, patients using MAT as part of treatment may feel shameful about using this type of medication, leaving them at a very high risk for relapse if they abruptly discontinue the medication. What can make things worse for these patients is that because of the high correlation between past experiences of trauma and opioid use, being rejected or shamed by a recovery group may also retraumatize these patients. This shame is a huge barrier to their treatment and leaves them very vulnerable to relapse if they return to opioid or any other drug use in an attempt to numb the unpleasant feelings this negative experience may bring back.

Because of the evidence supporting MAT, more medical and recovery professionals are beginning to consider the use of prescribed medication as an adjunct to evidence-based treatment and to be no different than using medications to treat other health conditions such as asthma or diabetes. Patients are using the medication under close medical supervision to support their recovery, not to get high. As noted in chapter 8, it can be helpful to focus on recovery as the "establishment of new behaviors" in this context, similar to recovery from other types of addiction, such as overeating or sexual addiction, where it is not possible to simply eliminate the behavior or substance.[10]

Medications commonly used in MAT include buprenorphine/naloxone and extended-release naltrexone. These medications have been shown to improve the likelihood of abstinence from opioids, boost retention and engagement in treatment, reduce cravings for opioids, and lower relapse rates.[11]

Educating patients to understand MAT as a tool to help them achieve recovery can counteract potential stigma from others—or self-directed stigma patients may feel about using medications. Preparing patients for dealing with stigma can also help reduce its impact. To do this, counselors may warn patients of the possibility that negative views about MAT may be voiced at support group meetings. Patients can also be reminded about boundaries and how it is up to them to decide what, if anything, they want to disclose about their use of medication. Ideally, counselors will be able to direct patients to groups that are accepting of MAT. Locating opioid-specific groups, either in person or online, can be especially helpful. This is not always possible due to the lack of a centralized structure for peer support groups and will vary greatly from one locality to another.

Patient Case: James in Outpatient Treatment Experiences Stigma at a Narcotics Anonymous Group Meeting

James is a thirty-six-year-old man doing well in outpatient treatment for opioid use disorder. This is James's second time in treatment. His treatment protocol includes MAT, using the medication buprenorphine. He feels ready to try a peer support group and attends an NA meeting. When James returns to his next treatment group session, he tells his counselor that he started feeling shameful about his medication use after the meeting.

James reported that several NA group members voiced strong negative opinions about the use of medications and said that anyone taking a medication like buprenorphine is not really "clean and sober" and is in fact still an "addict." James said he left the meeting feeling very low self-esteem, and his motivation to continue his current treatment program just plummeted, despite the positive results he had been experiencing with his counselor. That evening, James decides to stop taking his medication, without telling his counselor. Two days later, he relapses and begins using heroin again. This is especially troubling because opioid patients such as James who relapse and return to using the same amount of drugs they had been using can easily overdose due to their lowered tolerance level during periods of abstinence.

The Challenge for Clinicians

The challenge for clinicians is in helping patients find appropriate peer support groups where their medication use will be understood and accepted as part of treatment. All patients with opioid use disorders can benefit from attending an opioid-specific support group. Participation in opioid-specific support groups during inpatient treatment and throughout outpatient treatment into long-term recovery has been proven to be a critical factor in maintaining abstinence for the long term. Such specialized groups can also offer opportunities for psychosocial education, like role-plays to help patients practice addressing stigma or disclosing a comfortable amount of detail regarding their medication use.[12] Patients should be prepared to try more than one group before they find one that feels comfortable and safe.

Unfortunately, as James's story shows, encountering an unwelcoming group can be tremendously painful. As Stone explains, being criticized for taking medication "is super-demoralizing to somebody, especially when they're working so hard against an addiction that is so challenging to overcome. We've had patients that were just asked to leave the meeting altogether and told that they couldn't even participate." As noted earlier, it is very common for opioid patients in particular to have experiences of trauma in their background. Experiencing trauma can impact patients' ability to form trusting relationships and damage their sense of self, with many people feeling an intense sense of shame or guilt about what happened to them. "They have a history of being told not to trust themselves, not to trust their own intuition," says Stone. "[Then] they go into a meeting where the people there are telling them that they're not sober, that they're still in active addiction, that they can't talk at a meeting because they're basically high right now, and nothing that comes out of their mouth can be valuable or worthwhile to anybody else, and they just need to sit and listen. That can retraumatize somebody."

What You Can Do

Due to the potential difficulty of finding appropriate peer support, Stone says it's important to set realistic expectations about peer support groups and let patients know they don't have to accept a situation that makes them feel bad. "I don't want them to get the message from me that you're going to go to meetings, you're going to get a sponsor, you're going to do all these things, it's gonna be great, and they go and they feel judged and shamed," she says.

Counselors can educate patients so they understand clearly that MAT is a tool to support their recovery, not a crutch. "We try to help patients understand that the use of medication to treat somebody in their addiction is part of abstinence, [as valid] as other medications used in medical settings," says Stone. "Many medications can be abused, but when they're part of a treatment protocol, they equate to that patient maintaining their abstinence. That's how we feel about the use of this medication for our patients. They are maintaining their abstinence. They are taking something prescribed, something for their health, as part of their treatment process."

When possible, connect patients with a group specifically created for opioid use disorder. You may need to have staff or peers recommend and vet local groups before sending patients. Some local areas may have greater awareness of MAT and have more options for opioid-specific peer recovery groups, but that will vary because there is no central leadership or system of "policing" peer groups. Furthermore, groups such as NA may actually be more likely to assert negative views about medication use and may be more likely to directly question a new member about it because they are more knowledgeable, whereas an AA group may not even be aware of the issue.

Some treatment facilities have started their own on-site peer recovery meetings with a statement declaring all patients are welcome regardless of their medication use. This can communicate an accepting tone that encourages a larger community to attend while still remaining MAT-positive. Organizations such as LifeRing Secular Recovery, SMART Recovery, Women for Sobriety, and Methadone Anonymous can be helpful, as many offer physical peer-to-peer support meetings and some offer online forums or chat groups. More about these groups is included in the resources section in Appendix B in this guide.

As Stone explains, the goal is to direct patients in MAT to peer support meetings where they feel "welcomed with open arms and they're going to experience the same sense of support that anybody else would experience, even if they are on buprenorphine." It is also important to keep in mind that groups may change from day to day, depending on who attends. Even a group that felt supportive one day can have a member appear who voices negative opinions, and "unless the members pull that person aside and go, 'Hey, man, you've got to keep those opinions to yourself,' then that becomes part of the picture of that meeting."

In treatment, be sure to address the potential MAT stigma a patient might encounter in some peer support groups. This can help patients be educated about the issue and can open up a line of communication with the counselor. As Stone explains, "I want a patient to tell me if this happens. I want to stay aware of what they experience at meetings so that I can compassionately empathize with them." If a patient is caught totally off guard by being asked if they use medication, or by being criticized for it, the shame they feel may keep them from talking with their counselor or anyone else about the issue.

Stone also stresses the importance of discussing boundaries and reminding patients that they can wait to share information with people only after they have shown themselves to be trustworthy. "They don't have to tell anybody what kind of medications they're on. That's information that they get to decide to share with somebody who's deserving of that information."

CREATE AN OPIOID-SPECIFIC SUPPORT GROUP

Creating a support group specifically for patients with opioid use disorder can be especially helpful. A weekly meeting facilitated by a mental health counselor, alcohol and drug counselor, or trained peer coach can be incorporated into inpatient and outpatient treatment and can carry on during continuing care. Such a group can be a safe place where patients can learn from each other's challenges, can celebrate each other's victories, and can include members who use medications and some who don't. A setting like this can give MAT patients a chance to discuss their experiences taking medications such as buprenorphine/naloxone or naltrexone and to receive help and guidance from peers who understand because they also have opioid use disorders. Connecting patients to program alumni or online support groups can also help them find an inclusive environment that offers acceptance, support, and encouragement. Peer support resources can be found in Appendix B in this guide.

▨ ▨ ▨

Screening, Assessment, and Diagnostic Tools

(Entries shown in a gray box indicate opioid-specific resources.)

Screening Tools

CAGE Questionnaire

The CAGE questionnaire[1] is an easy-to-use, four-question screening test for problem drinking and potential alcohol problems. It can be self-administered or administered by a health care professional.

Center for Adolescent Substance Abuse Research (CeASAR) CRAFFT

The CRAFFT screening tool is a behavioral health screening tool for use with children and young adults under the age of twenty-one and is recommended by the American Academy of Pediatrics Committee on Substance Abuse for use with adolescents. It consists of a series of six questions developed to screen adolescents for high-risk alcohol and other drug use disorders simultaneously. It is a short, effective screening tool meant to assess whether a longer conversation about the context of use, frequency, and other risks and consequences of alcohol and other drug use is warranted. Learn more at www.ceasar-boston .org/CRAFFT.

Drug Abuse Screening Test (DAST)

DAST-10 is a ten-item brief screening tool to assess drug use, not including alcohol or tobacco use, in the past twelve months. The ten-item tool has been condensed from the twenty-eight-item DAST and should take less than eight minutes to complete. The tool can be administered by a clinician or self-administered by the patient. Learn more at www.drugabuse.gov[2] or at www.samhsa.gov.[3]

NIDA Drug Screening Tool, NIDA-Modified ASSIST (NM ASSIST)

The NM ASSIST screening tool was created for use in general medical settings. It asks a series of questions to identify risky substance use in adult patients. The goal of the tool is to identify early drug use and prevent the escalation to addiction, to identify patients in need and refer them to specialty treatment, and to increase awareness of dangerous interactions between substance use and the patient's medical care, including dangerous drug interactions. Learn more at www.drugabuse.gov/nmassist.

Current Opioid Misuse Measure (COMM)

COMM is a seventeen-item patient self-assessment measure designed to identify those patients with chronic pain taking opioids who have indicators of current aberrant drug-related behaviors. Learn more at https://www.opioidrisk.com.

Opioid Risk Tool (ORT)

This brief self-report screening tool is designed for use with adult patients in primary care settings to assess risk for opioid abuse among individuals considering prescribed opioids for treatment of chronic pain. The tool should be administered to patients upon initial visit prior to beginning opiate pain management. Patients categorized as high risk are at increased likelihood of future abusive drug-related behavior. The ORT can be administered and scored in less than one minute and has been validated in both male and female patients, but not in non-pain populations. Find the tool at www.drugabuse.gov /sites/default/files/files/OpioidRiskTool.pdf.

Screener and Opioid Assessment for Patients with Pain (SOAPP-R)

The SOAPP-R takes five minutes to administer and score and predicts possible opioid abuse in chronic pain patients. It provides excellent discrimination between high-risk and low-risk patients.[4] The SOAPP-R is the revised version based on the SOAPP. Learn more at https://www.opioidrisk.com.

TCU Drug Screen 5

This seventeen-question screening instrument includes specific questions about individuals' frequency of, purpose for, and methods of opioid use. This is designed to inform more rapid and more accurate judgments about treatment referral. The screening tool is available to addiction treatment and criminal justice professionals. It was developed by researchers at Texas Christian University's Institute of Behavioral Research and the Center for Health and Justice. Find the screening tool at https://ibr.tcu.edu/forms/.

Assessment Tools

Addiction Severity Index (ASI)

The ASI is a widely utilized measure for assessing problem severity in seven areas commonly affected by alcohol and drug misuse: (1) medical status, (2) employment and support, (3) drug use, (4) alcohol use, (5) legal status, (6) family/social status, and (7) psychiatric status. Its easy-to-administer format and its measurement of related life domains provide treatment providers with a useful tool to assess patients at intake as well as throughout treatment. The ASI-MV (Addiction Severity Index-Multimedia Version) is the electronic version of the traditional paper-and-pencil-administered ASI. The BHI-MV (Behavioral Health Index-Multimedia Version) is a similar online behavioral health assessment tool that provides an overview of the patient's functioning, asking questions about broader areas of mental health issues, eating disorders, trauma, self-harm, tobacco use, and others. Both the ASI-MV and BHI-MV include automatic scoring and reports, are available in both English and Spanish, and can be found at www.hazelden.org/bookstore.

The Clinical Institute Narcotic Assessment (CINA)

The CINA Scale for Withdrawal Symptoms measures eleven signs and symptoms commonly seen in patients during narcotic withdrawal. This helps gauge the severity of symptoms and monitor changes in clinical status over time.

Clinical Opiate Withdrawal Scale (COWS)

COWS measures eleven items and is very similar to the CINA assessment. COWS is commonly used in clinical practice but has not been systematically validated. CINA is a validated tool. Research shows that both the CINA and COWS are well suited for assessing and tracking opioid withdrawal.[5]

Objective Opiate Withdrawal Scale (OOWS)

OOWS contains thirteen physically observable signs, rated present or absent, based on a timed, brief period of observation of the patient by a rater.

Subjective Opiate Withdrawal Scale (SOWS)

SOWS contains sixteen symptoms for the patient to rate in intensity, asking how he or she "feels now," including feeling anxious, perspiring, feeling like vomiting, having hot flashes, and several more symptoms.

Working Alliance Inventory-Short Revised (WAI-SR)

The WAI-SR is a twelve-item measure of the therapeutic alliance between patient and counselor that assesses three key aspects of the alliance: (a) agreement on the tasks of therapy, (b) agreement on the goals of therapy, and (c) development of an affective bond.[6] Learn more at wai.profhorvath.com.

Patient Motivation and Readiness Rating Tools

The Stages of Change Readiness and Treatment Eagerness Scale (SOCRATES)

The SOCRATES assessment tool[7] is designed to assess readiness for change in individuals who have a problem with alcohol or other drugs. Version 8 of the assessment offers nineteen items that ask a patient to rate how he or she currently feels about his or her current drug use. Scores fall into three categories: recognition, ambivalence, or taking steps. This is a public domain instrument and may be used without special permission. The assessment tool and scoring can be found in SAMHSA TIP 35: *Enhancing Motivation for Change in Substance Abuse Treatment.*[8] You can obtain a free copy of TIP 35 at www.samhsa.gov.

Alcohol (and Illegal Drugs) Decisional Balance Scale

The Alcohol (and Illegal Drugs) Decisional Balance Scale asks patients to rate twenty items that ask about their drinking or other drug use along a continuum from "Not important at all" to "Extremely important." The assessment tool and scoring can be found in SAMHSA TIP 35: *Enhancing Motivation for Change in Substance Abuse Treatment.*[9] You can obtain a free copy of TIP 35 at www.samhsa.gov.

University of Rhode Island Change Assessment (URICA)

The URICA tool can be used to assess an individual's willingness to change by asking a patient to rate how he or she feels about approaching problems in his or her life. When the "problem" is alcohol or other drug use, patients are asked to answer with regard to how they feel about problems related to their drug use. Scores fall into precontemplation, contemplation, participation (action), and maintenance.

There are several versions of URICA that range from a twelve-item version to a thirty-two-item version. The tool can be used when a patient is entering treatment for a substance use disorder. It can also be used to indicate progress during treatment (in this case the action and maintenance subscale scores are used rather than the readiness score). More information can be found in a research study by DiClemente.[10] The assessment tool and scoring can be found in SAMHSA TIP 35: *Enhancing Motivation for Change in Substance Abuse Treatment.*[11] You can obtain a free copy of TIP 35 at www.samhsa.gov.

Diagnostic Tools and Level of Service Guidelines

Diagnostic and Statistical Manual of Mental Disorders (DSM-5)

The American Psychiatric Association's fifth edition of the *Diagnostic and Statistical Manual of Mental Disorders (DSM-5)* is a manual used by behavioral health professionals, such as psychiatrists and psychologists, as a guide to diagnosing people with substance use and mental health disorders. *DSM-5* defines the diagnosis of substance use disorders as mild, moderate, or severe, as determined by the number of diagnostic criteria met by an individual. Learn more at www.dsm5.org.

American Society of Addiction Medicine (ASAM) Criteria

The ASAM criteria assess patients using six dimensions to create a holistic, biopsychosocial assessment for service planning and treatment across all services and levels of care. The ASAM criteria are the most widely used and comprehensive set of guidelines for placement, continued stay, and transfer/discharge of patients with addiction and co-occurring conditions. ASAM's criteria are required in a majority of the states in the United States. Learn more at www.asam.org.

Peer Support Resources

MAT-Friendly Peer Support

LifeRing Secular Recovery

LifeRing Secular Recovery is an abstinence-based worldwide network of individuals seeking to live in recovery from addiction to alcohol or other nonmedically indicated drugs. LifeRing offers peer-to-peer support meetings in the United States, Canada, and other selected countries of the world. The LifeRing site includes a meeting finder to help find a physical meeting location near you. They also have online meetings using chat room technology. Learn more at www.lifering.org.

Medication-Assisted Recovery Services (MARS)

Since 2005, the Medication-Assisted Recovery Services program (a peer-initiated and peer-based recovery support project) has worked to inspire the transformation of medication-assisted treatment into medication-assisted recovery. The project was initiated by a group of methadone maintenance patients, as well as other individuals who play an essential role in the field of methadone maintenance. It is MARS's mission to provide peer support services and training to the medication-assisted recovery community. They design, implement, and evaluate selected peer-delivered recovery support services to complement existing treatment programs. Learn more at www.marsproject.org.

National Alliance for Medication Assisted Recovery (NAMA-R)

The National Alliance for Medication Assisted Recovery is an organization of medication-assisted treatment (MAT) patients, health care professionals, friends, and associates working together for greater public understanding and acceptance of MAT. They work to fight stigma and discrimination in patients using MAT and offer education and success stories of using MAT in treatment of substance use disorders. Learn more at www.methadone.org.

SMART Recovery

SMART Recovery is a recovery support group for people healing from substance use disorders. SMART Recovery supports the scientifically informed use of psychological treatment and legally prescribed psychiatric and addiction medications. They sponsor face-to-face meetings around the world, offer daily online meetings, and have an online message board and chat room. Learn more at www.smartrecovery.org.

Women for Sobriety (WFS)

Women for Sobriety, Inc., is a nonprofit organization dedicated to helping women discover an abstinent new life. It is one of the first self-help recovery programs based on the emotional needs of women. Women for Sobriety has certified moderators leading face-to-face groups in the United States and Canada. They also have an online forum and weekly online chat group. Learn more at www.womenforsobriety.org.

Twelve Step Peer Support

Alcoholics Anonymous (AA)

Alcoholics Anonymous is an international fellowship of men and women who have had a drinking problem. Membership is open to anyone who wants to do something about his or her drinking problem. Meetings are available worldwide. Learn more about AA or find a meeting near your location using the meeting finder at www.aa.org.

Narcotics Anonymous (NA)

Narcotics Anonymous is the Twelve Step self-help group for individuals who have a desire to stop using drugs. The website includes contact information regarding local groups. Learn more at www.na.org.

Suggested Education Resources

American Academy of Addiction Psychiatry

The American Academy of Addiction Psychiatry offers information in the field of addiction psychiatry and encourages research on the etiology, prevention, identification, and treatment of substance use disorders. Learn more at www.aaap.org.

American Society of Addiction Medicine

The American Society of Addiction Medicine is a medical specialty society dedicated to educating physicians and improving the treatment of individuals with substance-related disorders. It provides numerous publications for physicians regarding substance-related disorder treatment. Learn more at www.asam.org.

Butler Center for Research

The Butler Center for Research at the Hazelden Betty Ford Foundation works to support sustained recovery from the disease of addiction by advancing knowledge about addiction, treatment, and recovery and by integrating addiction treatment research into practice. Find journal articles, treatment statistics, and trends, or search the library database on any addiction-related topic. Learn more at www.hazeldenbettyford .org/education/bcr.

NAADAC

NAADAC, the Association for Addiction Professionals, provides education, clinical training, and certification in addiction counseling to help counselors provide the highest quality and most up-to-date science-based services to patients, families, and communities. Among the organization's national certification programs are the National Certified Addiction Counselor and the Master Addiction Counselor designations. Learn more at www.naadac.org.

National Institute on Drug Abuse

The National Institute on Drug Abuse has a wealth of written and audiovisual materials—including patient handouts—on addictive substances, substance use disorder treatment, treatment research, and related issues, such as substance-related medical problems. Learn more at www.drugabuse.gov.

National Suicide Prevention Lifeline

The National Suicide Prevention Lifeline is a national network of local crisis centers that provides free and confidential emotional support to people in suicidal crisis or emotional distress twenty-four hours a day, seven days a week. They offer voice calls or online chat with a suicide prevention specialist. Call 1-800-273-8255 or visit www.suicidepreventionlifeline.org.

National Survey on Drug Use and Health (NSDUH)

NSDUH provides national and state-level data on the use of tobacco, alcohol, illicit drugs (including nonmedical use of prescription drugs), and mental health in the United States. NSDUH is sponsored by the Substance Abuse and Mental Health Services Administration (SAMHSA), an agency in the U.S. Department of Health and Human Services (DHHS). Learn more at nsduhweb.rti.org.

Screening, Brief Intervention, and Referral to Treatment (SBIRT)

SBIRT is a comprehensive, integrated public health approach to the delivery of early intervention and treatment services for persons with substance use disorders, as well as those at risk for developing these disorders. SAMHSA offers online resources designed to help implement SBIRT initiatives. Learn more at www.samhsa.gov/sbirt.

Online Publications

(Entries shown in a gray box indicate opioid-specific resources.)

SAMHSA TIPs

Treatment Improvement Protocols (TIPs) offer best practice guidelines for addiction treatment. The range of topics developed as TIPs is very broad and includes assessment and screening, enhancing motivation for change, specific populations (such as youth, older adults), specific drugs (such as stimulants, opioids, marijuana), and others. Examples of a few SAMHSA TIPs are listed below. Download a free copy of any TIP at samhsa.gov.

SAMHSA: A Collaborative Approach to the Treatment of Pregnant Women with Opioid Use Disorders (October 2016)

This manual offers best practices on collaborative treatment approaches for pregnant women living with opioid use disorders, and the risks and benefits associated with MAT. This manual is published under Practice and Policy Considerations for Child Welfare, Collaborating Medical and Service Providers. Download a free copy at https://store.samhsa.gov/product/A-Collaborative-Approach-to-the-Treatment -of-Pregnant-Women-with-Opioid-Use-Disorders/SMA16-4978.

SAMHSA TIP 35: Enhancing Motivation for Change in Substance Abuse Treatment

TIP 35[1] offers clear guidance on motivational approaches in clinical practice of treatment in people with substance use disorders. Motivation for change is a key component in addressing substance abuse. The results of longitudinal research suggest that an individual's level of motivation is a very strong predictor of whether the individual's substance use will change or remain the same. Motivation-enhancing techniques are associated with increased participation in treatment and improved treatment outcomes. Learn more by downloading a free copy of TIP 35 at www.samhsa.gov.

SAMHSA TIP 45: Detoxification and Substance Abuse Treatment

TIP 45[2] educates substance use counselors and clinicians about detoxification and withdrawal, including guidelines related to specific substances (alcohol, opioids, stimulants, inhalants, marijuana, club drugs, and more). It addresses patient placement, detox services for specific substances, co-occurring disorders, financing issues, and screening and assessment tools. Learn more by downloading a free copy of TIP 45 at www.samhsa.gov.

SAMHSA List of Trauma-Specific Interventions

SAMHSA has compiled a list with links to information about well-known Trauma-Specific Interventions based on psychosocial educational empowerment principles that have been used extensively in public system settings. These include the ATRIUM model, Sanctuary Model, Seeking Safety, and others. Learn more at www.samhsa.gov/nctic/trauma-interventions.

NOTES

Acknowledgments

1. Nearly 70 percent of patients were successfully induced on one of the medications during residential treatment: 34 percent (n = 87) on buprenorphine and 35 percent (n = 92) on naltrexone. Among patients on naltrexone, 71 percent took the intramuscular extended-release version (Vivitrol) and 29 percent took the oral formulation.

Chapter 1: Understanding Opioids

1. Drug Enforcement Administration, "DEA Issues Carfentanil Warning to Police and Public: Dangerous Opioid 10,000 Times More Potent Than Morphine and 100 Times More Potent Than Fentanyl," news release, September 22, 2016, https://www.dea.gov/divisions/hq/2016/hq092216 .shtml.

2. National Institute on Drug Abuse, "Overdose Death Rates," revised September 2017, https:// www.drugabuse.gov/related-topics/trends-statistics/overdose-death-rates.

3. "Comprehensive Opioid Response with the 12 Steps (COR-12): Hazelden's Treatment Response to the Opioid Epidemic," white paper (Center City, MN: Hazelden, 2012).

4. American Society of Addiction Medicine, "Opioid Addiction 2016 Facts and Figures," https:// www.asam.org/docs/default-source/advocacy/opioid-addiction-disease-facts-figures.pdf, which references Center for Behavioral Health Statistics and Quality, *Key Substance Use and Mental Health Indicators in the United States: Results from the 2015 National Survey on Drug Use and Health*, HHS Publication No. SMA 16-4984, NSDUH Series H-51 (Rockville, MD: Center for Behavioral Health Statistics and Quality, Substance Abuse and Mental Health Services Administration, 2016), http://www.samhsa.gov/data.

5. Excerpted from American Society of Addiction Medicine, "Opioid Addiction 2016 Facts and Figures," https://www.asam.org/docs/default-source/advocacy/opioid-addiction-disease-facts-figures.pdf, which references R. A. Rudd, P. Seth, F. David, and L. Scholl, "Increases in Drug and Opioid-Involved Overdose Deaths—United States, 2010–2015," *Morbidity and Mortality Weekly Report* 65 (2016): 1445–1452, doi:10.15585/mmwr.mm655051e1.

6. Excerpted from American Society of Addiction Medicine, "Opioid Addiction 2016 Facts and Figures," https://www.asam.org/docs/default-source/advocacy/opioid-addiction-disease-facts-figures.pdf, which references R. A. Rudd, P. Seth, F. David, and L. Scholl, "Increases in Drug and Opioid-Involved Overdose Deaths—United States, 2010–2015," *Morbidity and Mortality Weekly Report* 65 (2016): 1445–1452, doi:10.15585/mmwr.mm655051e1.

7. Centers for Disease Control and Prevention, "Understanding the Epidemic," page last updated August 30, 2017, https://www.cdc.gov/drugoverdose/epidemic/index.html.

8. Centers for Disease Control and Prevention, "Understanding the Epidemic," page last updated August 30, 2017, https://www.cdc.gov/drugoverdose/epidemic/index.html.

9. C. S. Florence, C. Zhou, F. Luo, and L. Xu, "The Economic Burden of Prescription Opioid Overdose, Abuse, and Dependence in the United States, 2013," *Medical Care* 54 (2016): 901–906, doi:10.1097 /MLR.0000000000000625, quoted in W. M. Compton, "Research on the Use and Misuse of Fentanyl and Other Synthetic Opioids," June 30, 2017, https://www.drugabuse.gov/about-nida/legislative -activities/testimony-to-congress/2017/research-use-misuse-fentanyl-other-synthetic-opioids.

10. Science Daily, "Costs of US Prescription Opioid Epidemic Estimated at $78.5 Billion," September 14, 2016, https://www.sciencedaily.com/releases/2016/09/160914105756.htm.

11. K. L. Hahn, "Strategies to Prevent Opioid Misuse, Abuse, and Diversion That May Also Reduce the Associated Costs," *American Health and Drug Benefits* 4, no. 2 (2011): 107–114, https:// www.ncbi.nlm.nih.gov/pmc/articles/PMC4106581.

12. Coalition Against Insurance Fraud, *Prescription for Peril* (Washington, DC: Coalition Against Insurance Fraud, December 2007), 4–5, www.insurancefraud.org/downloads/drugDiversion.pdf.

13. Centers for Disease Control and Prevention, "HIV Among People Who Inject Drugs," page last updated February 22, 2018, https://www.cdc.gov/hiv/group/hiv-idu.html.

14. Centers for Disease Control and Prevention, "Prescription Opioids," page last updated August 29, 2017, https://www.cdc.gov/drugoverdose/opioids/prescribed.html.

15. Centers for Disease Control and Prevention, "CDC Launches Campaign to Help States Fight Prescription Opioid Epidemic," press release, September 25, 2017, https://www.cdc.gov/media /releases/2017/p0925-rx-awareness-campaigns.html.

16. Centers for Disease Control and Prevention, "Policy Impact: Prescription Painkiller Overdoses," November 2011, https://www.cdc.gov/drugoverdose/pdf/policyimpact-prescriptionpainkillerod-a.pdf.

17. National Institute on Drug Abuse, "Prescription Opioids and Heroin," page last updated January 2018, https://www.drugabuse.gov/publications/research-reports/relationship-between -prescription-drug-heroin-abuse/prescription-opioid-use-risk-factor-heroin-use.

18. National Institute on Drug Abuse, "Prescription and Over-the-Counter Medications," revised November 2015, https://www.drugabuse.gov/publications/drugfacts/prescription-over-counter -medications.

19. National Institute on Drug Abuse for Teens, "Prescription Drugs," revised March 2017, https:// teens.drugabuse.gov/drug-facts/prescription-drugs.

20. A. M. Young, J. R. Havens, and C. G. Leukefeld, "Route of Administration for Illicit Prescription Opioids: A Comparison of Rural and Urban Drug Users," *Harm Reduction Journal* 7, no. 24 (2010), doi:10.1186/1477-7517-7-24.

21. Drug Enforcement Administration, "DEA Issues Carfentanil Warning to Police and Public: Dangerous Opioid 10,000 Times More Potent Than Morphine and 100 Times More Potent Than Fentanyl," news release, September 22, 2016, https://www.dea.gov/divisions/hq/2016/hq092216 .shtml.

22. J. Suzuki and S. El-Haddad, "A Review: Fentanyl and Non-pharmaceutical Fentanyls," *Drug and Alcohol Dependence* 171 (2017): 107–116, doi:10.1016/j.drugalcdep.2016.11.033.

23. National Institute on Drug Abuse, "Overdose Death Rates," revised September 2017, https:// www.drugabuse.gov/related-topics/trends-statistics/overdose-death-rates.

24. Centers for Disease Control and Prevention, "Increases in Drug and Opioid Overdose Deaths— United States 2000–2014," *Morbidity and Mortality Weekly Report* 64, no. 50 (2016): 1378–1382, https://www.cdc.gov/mmwr/preview/mmwrhtml/mm6450a3.htm.

25. W. M. Compton, "Research on the Use and Misuse of Fentanyl and Other Synthetic Opioids," June 30, 2017, https://www.drugabuse.gov/about-nida/legislative-activities/testimony-to -congress/2017/research-use-misuse-fentanyl-other-synthetic-opioids.

26. R. M. Gladden, P. Martinez, and P. Seth, "Fentanyl Law Enforcement Submissions and Increases in Synthetic Opioid-Involved Overdose Deaths—27 States, 2013–2014," *Morbidity and Mortality Weekly Report* 65 (2016): 837–843, doi:10.15585/mmwr.mm6533a2, quoted in W. M. Compton, "Research on the Use and Misuse of Fentanyl and Other Synthetic Opioids," June 30, 2017, https://www.drugabuse.gov/about-nida/legislative-activities/testimony-to -congress/2017/research-use-misuse-fentanyl-other-synthetic-opioids.

27. A. D. Bode, M. Singh, J. Andrews, G. B. Kapur, and A. A. Baez, "Fentanyl Laced Heroin and Its Contribution to a Spike in Heroin Overdose in Miami-Dade County," *American Journal of Emergency Medicine* 35, no. 9 (2017): 1364–1365, doi:10.1016/j.ajem.2017.02.043; Drug Enforcement Administration, "DEA Issues Carfentanil Warning to Police and Public," news release, September 22, 2016, https://www.dea.gov/divisions/hq/2016/hq092216.shtml; R. M. Gladden, P. Martinez, and P. Seth, "Fentanyl Law Enforcement Submissions and Increases in Synthetic Opioid-Involved Overdose Deaths—27 States, 2013–2014," *Morbidity and Mortality Weekly Report* 65 (2016): 837–843, doi:10.15585/mmwr.mm6533a2, quoted in W. M. Compton, "Research on the Use and Misuse of Fentanyl and Other Synthetic Opioids," June 30, 2017, https://www.drugabuse.gov/about-nida/legislative-activities/testimony-to-congress/2017/research-use-misuse -fentanyl-other-synthetic-opioids.

28. Substance Abuse and Mental Health Services Administration, "Opioids," last updated February 23, 2016, https://www.samhsa.gov/atod/opioids.

29. National Institute on Drug Abuse, "Heroin," page last updated March 2018, https://www .drugabuse.gov/publications/research-reports/heroin/what-heroin.

30. Centers for Disease Control and Prevention, "Vital Signs: Today's Heroin Epidemic—More People at Risk, Multiple Drugs Abused," page last updated July 7, 2015, https://www.cdc.gov /vitalsigns/heroin/index.html.

31. Centers for Disease Control and Prevention, "Heroin Overdose Data," page last updated January 26, 2017, www.cdc.gov/drugoverdose/data/heroin.html.

32. Substance Abuse and Mental Health Services Administration, *Results from the 2013 National Survey on Drug Use and Health: Summary of National Findings,* NSDUH Series H-48, HHS Publication No. (SMA) 14-4863 (Rockville, MD: Substance Abuse and Mental Health Services Administration, 2014).

33. Centers for Disease Control and Prevention, "Vital Signs: Today's Heroin Epidemic—More People at Risk, Multiple Drugs Abused," page last updated July 7, 2015, https://www.cdc.gov /vitalsigns/heroin/index.html.

34. W. M. Compton, "Research on the Use and Misuse of Fentanyl and Other Synthetic Opioids," June 30, 2017, https://www.drugabuse.gov/about-nida/legislative-activities/testimony-to-congress /2017/research-use-misuse-fentanyl-other-synthetic-opioids.

35. T. J. Cicero, M. S. Ellis, H. L. Surratt, and S. P. Kurtz, "The Changing Face of Heroin Use in the United States: A Retrospective Analysis of the Past 50 Years," *JAMA Psychiatry* 71, no. 7 (2014): 821–826, doi:10.1001/jamapsychiatry.2014.366.

36. SAMHSA Advisory Bulletin, February 7, 2014, http://www.samhsa.gov/newsroom/advisories /1402075426.aspx (page discontinued).

37. N. D. Volkow, "America's Addiction to Opioids: Heroin and Prescription Drug Abuse," May 14, 2014, https://www.drugabuse.gov/about-nida/legislative-activities/testimony-to-congress/2018 /americas-addiction-to-opioids-heroin-prescription-drug-abuse.

Chapter 2: Effects of Opioids on the Brain and Body

1. J. Upadhyay, N. Maleki, J. Potter, I. Elman, D. Rudrauf, J. Knudsen, D. Wallin, G. Pendse, L. McDonald, M. Griffin, J. Anderson, L. Nutile, P. Renshaw, R. Weiss, L. Becerra, and D. Borsook, "Alterations in Brain Structure and Functional Connectivity in Prescription Opioid-Dependent Patients," *Brain* 133, no. 7 (2010): 2098–2114, doi:10.1093/brain/awq138.

2. National Institute on Drug Abuse, "Heroin: What Are the Long-Term Effects of Heroin Use?," page last updated March 2018, https://www.drugabuse.gov/publications/research-reports/heroin /what-are-long-term-effects-heroin-use.

3. T. R. Kosten and T. P. George, "The Neurobiology of Opioid Dependence: Implications for Treatment," *Science and Practice Perspectives* 1, no. 1 (2002): 13–20.

4. H. Gutstein and H. Akil, "Opioid Analgesics," in *Goodman & Gilman's The Pharmacological Basis of Therapeutics*, 11th ed. (New York: McGraw-Hill, 2006), 547–590, quoted in "Misuse of Prescription Drugs," page last updated January 2018, https://www.drugabuse.gov/publications /research-reports/misuse-prescription-drugs/which-classes-prescription-drugs-are-commonly -misused.

5. U.S. National Library of Medicine: MedlinePlus, "Cerebral Hypoxia," originally published 2014, page last updated April 30, 2018, https://medlineplus.gov/ency/article/001435.htm, quoted in L. Brande, "Opioid Overdose," https://drugabuse.com/library/opioid-overdose.

6. V. E. Whiteman, J. L. Salemi, M. F. Mogos, M. A. Cain, M. H. Aliyu, and H. M. Salihu, "Maternal Opioid Drug Use during Pregnancy and Its Impact on Perinatal Morbidity, Mortality, and the Costs of Medical Care in the United States," *Journal of Pregnancy* 2014 (2014), doi:10.1155/2014/906723.

7. S. W. Patrick, R. E. Schumacher, B. D. Benneyworth, E. E. Krans, J. M. McAllister, and M. M. Davis, "Neonatal Abstinence Syndrome and Associated Health Care Expenditures: United States, 2000–2009," *Journal of the American Medical Association* 307, no. 18 (2012): 1934–1940, doi:10.1001/jama.2012.3951.

8. International Drug Policy Consortium, "Open Letter regarding Alarmist and Inaccurate Reporting on Prescription Opiate Use by Pregnant Women," March 11, 2013, http://idpc.net /alerts/2013/03/open-letter-regarding-alarmist-and-inaccurate-reporting-on-prescription -opiate-use-by-pregnant-women.

9. M. Lee, S. M. Silverman, H. Hansen, V. B. Patel, and L. Manchikanti, "A Comprehensive Review of Opioid-Induced Hyperalgesia," *Pain Physician* 14, no. 2 (2011): 145–161, quoted in National Institute on Drug Abuse, "Misuse of Prescription Drugs," page last updated January 2018, https://www.drugabuse.gov/publications/research-reports/misuse-prescription-drugs /which-classes-prescription-drugs-are-commonly-misused.

10. N. D. Volkow, G.-J. Wang, J. S. Fowler, D. Tomasi, and F. Telang, "Addiction: Beyond Dopamine Reward Circuitry," *Proceedings of the National Academy of Sciences* 108, no. 37 (2011): 15037–15042, doi:10.1073/pnas.1010654108.

11. National Institute on Drug Abuse, "Misuse of Prescription Drugs," page last updated January 2018, https://www.drugabuse.gov/publications/research-reports/misuse-prescription-drugs /which-classes-prescription-drugs-are-commonly-misused.

12. CNN Health, "Opioid Addiction Rates Continue to Skyrocket," June 29, 2017, http://www.cnn .com/2017/06/29/health/opioid-addiction-rates-increase-500/index.html.

13. L. Brande, "Opioid Overdose," https://drugabuse.com/library/opioid-overdose.

14. World Health Organization, "Information Sheet on Opioid Overdose," November 2014, www .who.int/substance_abuse/information_sheet/en/; Substance Abuse and Mental Health Services Administration, "Opioid Overdose," page last updated March 10, 2016, https://www.samhsa .gov/medication-assisted-treatment/treatment/opioid-overdose, both quoted in L. Brande, "Opioid Overdose," https://drugabuse.com/library/opioid-overdose.

15. "CDC Grand Rounds: Prescription Drug Overdoses—A U.S. Epidemic," *Morbidity and Mortality Weekly Report* 61, no. 1 (2012): 10–13, www.cdc.gov/mmwr/preview/mmwrhtml/mm6101a3.htm.

16. "CDC Grand Rounds: Prescription Drug Overdoses—A U.S. Epidemic," *Morbidity and Mortality Weekly Report* 61, no. 1 (2012): 10–13, www.cdc.gov/mmwr/preview/mmwrhtml/mm6101a3.htm.

17. "CDC Grand Rounds: Prescription Drug Overdoses—A U.S. Epidemic," *Morbidity and Mortality Weekly Report* 61, no. 1 (2012): 10–13, www.cdc.gov/mmwr/preview/mmwrhtml/mm6101a3.htm.

18. National Institute on Drug Abuse, "Overdose Death Rates," revised September 2017, https:// www.drugabuse.gov/related-topics/trends-statistics/overdose-death-rates.

19. National Institute on Drug Abuse, "Opioid Overdose Crisis," revised March 2018, https://www .drugabuse.gov/drugs-abuse/opioids/opioid-overdose-crisis.

20. Centers for Disease Control and Prevention, "Prescription Opioid Overdose Data," page last updated August 1, 2017, https://www.cdc.gov/drugoverdose/data/overdose.html.

21. Centers for Disease Control and Prevention, "Prescription Opioid Overdose Data," page last updated August 1, 2017, https://www.cdc.gov/drugoverdose/data/overdose.html.

22. E. M. Ossiander, "Using Textual Cause-of-Death Data to Study Drug Poisoning Deaths," *American Journal of Epidemiology* 179, no. 7 (April 2014): 884–894, doi:10.1093/aje/kwt333.

23. Centers for Disease Control and Prevention, "Policy Impact: Prescription Painkiller Overdoses," November 2011, https://www.cdc.gov/drugoverdose/pdf/policyimpact-prescription painkillerod-a.pdf.

24. World Health Organization, "WHO Model List of Essential Medicines (20th List)," March 2017 (Amended August 2017), http://www.who.int/medicines/publications/essentialmedicines/20th _EML2017_FINAL_amendedAug2017.pdf?ua=1.

Chapter 3: Opioids in Special Populations

1. Center for Behavioral Health Statistics and Quality, *Key Substance Use and Mental Health Indicators in the United States: Results from the 2015 National Survey on Drug Use and Health,* HHS Publication No. SMA 16-4984, NSDUH Series H-51 (Rockville, MD: Center for Behavioral Health Statistics and Quality, 2016), http://www.samhsa.gov/data.

2. Center for Behavioral Health Statistics and Quality, *Key Substance Use and Mental Health Indicators in the United States: Results from the 2015 National Survey on Drug Use and Health,* HHS Publication No. SMA 16-4984, NSDUH Series H-51 (Rockville, MD: Center for Behavioral Health Statistics and Quality, 2016), http://www.samhsa.gov/data.

3. R. J. Fortuna, B. W. Robbins, E. Caiola, M. Joynt, and J. S. Halterman, "Prescribing of Controlled Medications to Adolescents and Young Adults in the United States," *Pediatrics* 126, no. 6 (2010): 1108–1116, doi:10.1542/peds.2010-0791.

4. R. Miech, L. Johnston, P. M. O'Malley, K. M. Keyes, and K. Heard, "Prescription Opioids in Adolescence and Future Opioid Misuse," *Pediatrics* 136, no. 5 (2015), doi:10.1542/peds.2015-1364.

5. C. Saint Louis, "Surge in Narcotic Prescriptions for Pregnant Women," *New York Times*, April 13, 2014, https://nytimes.com/2014/04/15/science/surge-in-prescriptions-for-opioid-painkillers-for-pregnant-women.html.

6. V. N. Tolia, S. W. Patrick, M. M. Bennett, K. Murthy, J. Sousa, P. B. Smith, R. H. Clark, and A. R. Spitzer, "Increasing Incidence of the Neonatal Abstinence Syndrome in U.S. Neonatal ICUs," *New England Journal of Medicine* 372, no. 22 (2015): 2118–2126, doi:10.1056/NEJMsa1500439.

7. Substance Abuse and Mental Health Services Administration, *A Collaborative Approach to the Treatment of Pregnant Women with Opioid Use Disorders,* HHS Publication No. (SMA) 16-4978 (Rockville, MD: Substance Abuse and Mental Health Services Administration, 2016), http://store.samhsa.gov.

8. American College of Obstetricians and Gynecologists Committee on Health Care for Underserved Women and American Society of Addiction Medicine, "Opioid Abuse, Dependence, and Addiction in Pregnancy," ACOG committee opinion no. 524, *Obstetrics and Gynecology* 119, no. 5 (2012): 1070–1076, cited in *A Collaborative Approach to the Treatment of Pregnant Women with Opioid Use Disorders,* HHS Publication No. (SMA) 16-4978 (Rockville, MD: Substance Abuse and Mental Health Services Administration, 2016), http://store.samhsa.gov.

9. K. Kaltenbach and L. Finnegan, "Prevention and Treatment Issues for Pregnant Cocaine-Dependent Women and Their Infants," *Annals of the New York Academy of Sciences* 846, no. 1 (1998): 329–334, doi:10.1111/j.1749-6632.1998.tb09749.x.

10. H. E. Jones, K. E. O'Grady, D. Malfi, and M. Tuten, "Methadone Maintenance vs. Methadone Taper during Pregnancy: Maternal and Neonatal Outcomes," *American Journal of Addictions* 17, no. 5 (2008): 372–386, doi:10.1080/10550490802266276.

11. International Drug Policy Consortium, "Open Letter regarding Alarmist and Inaccurate Reporting on Prescription Opiate Use by Pregnant Women," March 11, 2013, http://idpc.net/alerts/2013/03/open-letter-regarding-alarmist-and-inaccurate-reporting-on-prescription-opiate-use-by-pregnant-women.

12. S. B. Brogly, K. A. Saia, A. Y. Walley, H. M. Du, and P. Sebastiani, "Prenatal Buprenorphine versus Methadone Exposure and Neonatal Outcomes: Systematic Review and Meta-Analysis," *American Journal of Epidemiology* 180, no. 7 (2014): 673–686, doi:10.1093/aje/kwu190.

13. Substance Abuse and Mental Health Services Administration, *A Collaborative Approach to the Treatment of Pregnant Women with Opioid Use Disorders,* HHS Publication No. (SMA) 16-4978 (Rockville, MD: Substance Abuse and Mental Health Services Administration, 2016), http://store.samhsa.gov.

14. Hazelden Foundation, Butler Center for Research, "Addiction and Mental Illness," Research Update, April 2000, https://peerta.acf.hhs.gov/sites/default/files/public/uploaded_files/Addiction%20and%20Mental%20Illness_LK-nh.pdf.

15. Buppractice, "Psychiatric Comorbidities with Opioid Dependence," https://www.buppractice.com/node/12391 (page discontinued).

16. Dartmouth Psychiatric Research Center, cited in Hazelden Betty Ford Foundation, "Co-occurring Disorders: Drug Abuse and Mental Health Issues Combined," www.hazelden.org/web/public/document/co-occurring-mental-illness-addiction.pdf.

Chapter 4: Overview of Treatment and Recovery

1. Office of National Drug Control Policy, "Prescription Opioid Misuse, Heroin, and Fentanyl," accessed January 4, 2018, https://www.whitehouse.gov/ondcp/key-issues/prescription-opioid-misuse.

2. Federal Register, "Establishing the President's Commission on Combating Drug Addiction and the Opioid Crisis," April 3, 2017, https://www.federalregister.gov/documents/2017/04/03/2017-06716/establishing-the-presidents-commission-on-combating-drug-addiction-and-the-opioid-crisis.

3. A. Klein, "What Does It Really Mean to Be Providing Medication-Assisted Treatment for Opioid Addiction?," Butler Center for Research White Paper, October 2017, http://www.hazeldenbettyford.org/education/bcr/addiction-research/medication-assisted-treatment-opioid-addiction-wp-1017.

4. J. Warren, A. Gelb, J. Horowitz, and J. Riordan, *One in 100: Behind Bars in America 2008* (Washington, DC: The Pew Center on the States, The Pew Charitable Trusts, 2008); G. A. Zarkin, L. J. Dunlap, B. Wedehase, and A. J. Cowell, "The Effect of Alternative Staff Time Data Collection Methods on Drug Treatment Service Cost Estimates," *Evaluation and Program Planning* 31 (2008): 427–435, both cited in *Principles of Drug Abuse Treatment for Criminal Justice Populations: A Research-Based Guide,* NIH Publication No. 11-5316 (Bethesda, MD: National Institute on Drug Abuse, 2014), https://www.drugabuse.gov/publications/principles-drug-abuse-treatment-criminal-justice-populations/what-role-medications-in-treating-substance-abusing.

5. National Institute on Drug Abuse, *Principles of Drug Abuse Treatment for Criminal Justice Populations: A Research-Based Guide,* NIH Publication No. 11-5316 (Bethesda, MD: National Institute on Drug Abuse, 2014), https://www.drugabuse.gov/publications/principles-drug-abuse-treatment-criminal-justice-populations/what-role-medications-in-treating-substance-abusing.

6. Substance Abuse and Mental Health Services Administration, "Medication-Assisted Treatment (MAT)," last updated February 7, 2018, https://www.samhsa.gov/medication-assisted-treatment.

Chapter 5: Screening and Evaluation

1. Substance Abuse and Mental Health Services Administration, *The NSDUH Report: How Young Adults Obtain Prescription Pain Relievers for Nonmedical Use* 39 (2006), cited in M. D. Seppala with M. E. Rose, *Prescription Painkillers: History, Pharmacology, and Treatment* (Center City, MN: Hazelden Publishing, 2010), 5–6.

2. W. Ling, D. R. Wesson, and D. E. Smith, "Prescription Opiate Abuse," in *Substance Abuse: A Comprehensive Textbook,* 4th ed., eds. J. H. Lowinson, P. Ruiz, R. B. Millman, and J. G. Langrod (Philadelphia: Lippincott, Williams and Wilkins, 2005), 459–468, cited in M. D. Seppala with M. E. Rose, *Prescription Painkillers: History, Pharmacology, and Treatment* (Center City, MN: Hazelden Publishing, 2010), 5–6.

3. N. D. Volkow, G.-J. Wang, J. S. Fowler, D. Tomasi, and F. Telang, "Addiction: Beyond Dopamine Reward Circuitry," *Proceedings of the National Academy of Sciences* 108 (2011): 15037–15042, doi:10.1073/pnas.1010654108.

4. National Institute on Drug Abuse, "Misuse of Prescription Drugs," page last updated January 2018, https://www.drugabuse.gov/publications/research-reports/misuse-prescription-drugs/which-classes-prescription-drugs-are-commonly-misused.

5. American Society of Addiction Medicine, "Resources: Definition of Addiction," April 12, 2011, https://www.asam.org/resources/definition-of-addiction.

Duplicating this page is illegal. Do not duplicate without the publisher's written permission.

111

6. American Psychiatric Association, *Diagnostic and Statistical Manual of Mental Disorders, 5th Edition* (Washington, DC: American Psychiatric Association, 2013), 541.

7. D. Dowell, T. M. Haegerich, and R. Chou, "CDC Guideline for Prescribing Opioids for Chronic Pain—United States, 2016," *Morbidity and Mortality Weekly Report* 65, no. 1 (2016): 1–49, doi:10.15585/mmwr.rr6501e1.

8. Agency for Healthcare Research and Quality, "Trends in Opioid-Related Hospitalizations," page last reviewed March 2018, https://www.ahrq.gov/news/opioid-hospitalization-map.html.

9. M. Durkin, "Primary Care Takes on Opioid Addiction," *ACP Internist,* October 2017, https://acpinternist.org/archives/2017/10/primary-care-takes-on-opioid-addiction.htm.

10. Substance Abuse and Mental Health Services Administration, "Buprenorphine Waiver Management," https://www.samhsa.gov/medication-assisted-treatment/buprenorphine-waiver-management.

Chapter 6: Effective Treatment of Opioid Use Disorder

1. Substance Abuse and Mental Health Services Administration, "Cost Offset of Treatment Services," April 2009, www.samhsa-gpra.samhsa.gov/CSAT/view/docs/SAIS_GPRA_CostOffset SubstanceAbuse.pdf (page discontinued).

2. American Society of Addiction Medicine, ed. D. Mee-Lee, *The ASAM Criteria: Treatment Criteria for Addictive, Substance-Related, and Co-Occurring Conditions* (Chevy Chase, MD: American Society of Addiction Medicine, 2013).

3. Chart adapted from A. Klein, "What Does It Really Mean to Be Providing Medication-Assisted Treatment for Opioid Addiction?," Butler Center for Research White Paper, October 2017, http://www.hazeldenbettyford.org/education/bcr/addiction-research/medication-assisted -treatment-opioid-addiction-wp-1017.

4. G. Smedslund, R. C. Berg, K. T. Hammerstrom, A. Steiro, K. A. Leiknes, H. M. Dahl, and K. Karlsen, "Motivational Interviewing for Substance Abuse," *Cochrane Database of Systematic Reviews* 5 (2011): Cd008063, doi:10.1002/14651858.CD008063.pub2.

5. Paragraph adapted from National Institute on Drug Abuse, "12-Step Facilitation Therapy (Alcohol, Stimulants, Opiates)," page last updated January 2018, https://www.drugabuse .gov/publications/principles-drug-addiction-treatment-research-based-guide-third-edition /evidence-based-approaches-to-drug-addiction-treatment/behavioral-4.

6. R. J. Meyers, H. G. Roozen, and J. E. Smith, "The Community Reinforcement Approach: An Update of the Evidence," *Alcohol Research & Health* 33, no. 4 (2011): 380–388.

7. S. T. Higgins, A. J. Budney, W. K. Bickel, F. E. Foerg, R. Donham, and G. J. Badger, "Incentives Improve Outcome in Outpatient Behavioral Treatment of Cocaine Dependence," *Archives of General Psychiatry* 51, no. 7 (1994): 568–576, doi:10.1001/archpsyc.1994.03950070060011; S. T. Higgins, C. J. Wong, G. J. Badger, D. E. H. Ogden, and R. L. Dantona, "Contingent Reinforcement Increases Cocaine Abstinence during Outpatient Treatment and 1 Year of Follow-Up," *Journal of Consulting and Clinical Psychology* 68, no. 1 (2000): 64–72, doi:10.1037/0022 -006X.68.1.64; M. Y. Iguchi, M. A. Belding, A. R. Morral, R. J. Lamb, and S. D. Husband, "Reinforcing Operants Other Than Abstinence in Drug Abuse Treatment: An Effective Alternative for Reducing Drug Use," *Journal of Consulting and Clinical Psychology* 65, no. 3 (1997): 421–428, doi:10.1037/0022-006X.65.3.421; N. M. Petry, B. Martin, J. L. Cooney, and H. R. Kranzler, "Give Them Prizes, and They Will Come: Contingency Management for Treatment of Alcohol Dependence," *Journal of Consulting and Clinical Psychology* 68, no. 2 (2000): 250–257, doi:10 .1037/0022-006X.68.2.250; R. A. Rawson, M. J. McCann, F. Flammino, S. Shoptaw, K. Miotto,

C. Reiber, and W. Ling, "A Comparison of Contingency Management and Cognitive-Behavioral Approaches for Stimulant-Dependent Individuals," *Addiction* 101, no. 2 (2006): 267–274, doi:10 .1111/j.1360-0443.2006.01312.x.

8. S. T. Higgins and K. Silverman, *Motivating Illicit Drug Abusers to Change Their Behavior: Research on Contingency Management Interventions* (Washington, DC: American Psychological Association, 1999); S. T. Higgins, J. W. Tidey, and M. L. Stitzer, "Community Reinforcement and Contingency Management Interventions," in *Principles of Addiction Medicine,* 2nd ed., eds. A. W. Graham, T. K. Schultz, and B. B. Wilford (Chevy Chase, MD: American Society of Addiction Medicine, Inc., 1998), 675–690, both cited in S. T. Higgins and N. M. Petry, "Contingency Management: Incentives for Sobriety," *Alcohol Research & Health* 23, no. 2 (1999), https://pubs.niaaa .nih.gov/publications/arh23-2/122-127.pdf.

9. T. W. Menza, D. R. Jameson, J. P. Hughes, G. N. Colfax, S. Shoptaw, and M. R. Golden, "Contingency Management to Reduce Methamphetamine Use and Sexual Risk among Men Who Have Sex with Men: A Randomized Controlled Trial," *BMC Public Health* 10, no. 774 (2010), doi:10.1186/1471-2458-10-774; N. K. Lee and R. A. Rawson, "A Systematic Review of Cognitive and Behavioural Therapies for Methamphetamine Dependence," *Drug and Alcohol Review* 27, no. 3 (2008): 309–317, doi:10.1080/09595230801919494.

10. The PEW Charitable Trusts, "Medication-Assisted Treatment Improves Outcomes for Patients with Opioid Use Disorder: A Fact Sheet," November 22, 2016, http://www.pewtrusts.org/en/ research-and-analysis/fact-sheets/2016/11/medication-assisted-treatment-improves-outcomes -for-patients-with-opioid-use-disorder; Substance Abuse and Mental Health Services Administration, "Co-occurring Disorders," 2016, https://www.samhsa.gov/disorders/co-occurring, both cited in A. Klein, "What Does It Really Mean to Be Providing Medication-Assisted Treatment for Opioid Addiction?," Butler Center for Research White Paper, October 2017, http://www. hazeldenbettyford.org/education/bcr/addiction-research/medication-assisted-treatment-opioid -addiction-wp-1017.

11. Substance Abuse and Mental Health Services Administration, "Naltrexone," last updated September 12, 2016, https://www.samhsa.gov/medication-assisted-treatment/treatment/naltrexone.

12. Center for Substance Abuse Treatment, *Detoxification and Substance Abuse Treatment,* Treatment Improvement Protocol (TIP) Series No. 45, HHS Publication No. SMA 15-4131 (Rockville, MD: Center for Substance Abuse Treatment, 2006).

13. J. H. Donroe, S. R. Holt, and J. M. Tetrault, "Caring for Patients with Opioid Use Disorder in the Hospital," *CMAJ* 188, no. 17–18 (2016): 1232–1239, doi:10.1503/cmaj.160290.

Chapter 7: Medications Used to Treat Opioid Use Disorder

1. E. V. Nunes, E. Krupitsky, W. Ling, J. Zummo, A. Memisoglu, B. L. Silverman, and D. R. Gastfriend, "Treating Opioid Dependence with Injectable Extended-Release Naltrexone (XR-NTX): Who Will Respond?" *Journal of Addiction Medicine* 9, no. 3 (2015): 238–243, doi:10.1097/ADM .0000000000000125.

2. Alcoholics Anonymous World Services, *Twelve Steps and Twelve Traditions* (New York: Alcoholics Anonymous World Services, 1952), 141.

3. K. MacDonald, K. Lamb, M. L. Thomas, and W. Khentigan, "Buprenorphine Maintenance Treatment of Opiate Dependence: Correlations Between Prescriber Beliefs and Practices," *Substance Use and Misuse* 51, no. 1 (2016): 85–90, doi:10.3109/10826084.2015.1089905.

4. R. P. Mattick, C. Breen, J. Kimber, and M. Davoli, "Methadone Maintenance Therapy versus No Opioid Replacement Therapy for Opioid Dependence," *Cochrane Database of Systematic Reviews* 3 (2009): CD002209, doi:10.1002/14651858.CD002209.pub2.

Chapter 8: MAT as an Integrated Evidence-Based Practice

1. American Society of Addiction Medicine, "Advancing Access to Addiction Medications," accessed May 11, 2017, http://www.asam.org/docs/default-source/advocacy/aaam_implications-for-opioid-addiction-treatment_final.

2. American Society of Addiction Medicine, "Advancing Access to Addiction Medications," accessed May 11, 2017, http://www.asam.org/docs/default-source/advocacy/aaam_implications-for-opioid-addiction-treatment_final.

3. M. McGovern, G. J. McHugo, R. E. Drake, G. Bond, and M. R. Merrens, *Implementing Evidence-Based Practices in Behavioral Health* (Center City, MN: Hazelden, 2013), 73.

4. Language in chart adapted from William L. White, *Narcotics Anonymous and the Pharmacotherapeutic Treatment of Opioid Addiction in the United States* (Philadelphia: Philadelphia Department of Behavioral Health and Intellectual Disability Services/Great Lakes Addiction Technology Transfer Center, 2011), 35, which cites Robert L. DuPont and Mark S. Gold, "Comorbidity and 'Self-Medication,'" *Journal of Addictive Diseases* 26, no. 1 (2007): 13–27.

5. Substance Abuse and Mental Health Services Administration, "Recovery and Recovery Support," last modified September 20, 2017, www.samhsa.gov/recovery.

Chapter 9: Continuing Care Planning

1. The Washington Circle, "Recovery Management: Continuing Care Following Acute Treatment," http://www.washingtoncircle.org/pdfs/8c1.pdf.

2. B. G. Bergman, B. B. Hoeppner, L. M. Nelson, V. Slaymaker, and J. F. Kelly, "The Effects of Continuing Care on Emerging Adult Outcomes Following Residential Addiction Treatment," *Drug and Alcohol Dependence* 153 (2015): 207–214, doi:10.1016/j.drugalcdep.2015.05.017.

3. W. L. White, "Recovery: The Next Frontier," *Counselor: The Magazine for Addiction Professionals* 5, no. 1 (2004): 18–21.

4. Adapted from *Living in Balance: Moving from a Life of Addiction to a Life of Recovery, Recovery Management Sessions* (Center City, MN: Hazelden Publishing, 2015).

5. W. L. White, M. Boyle, and D. Loveland, "Addiction as Chronic Disease: From Rhetoric to Clinical Application," *Alcoholism Treatment Quarterly* 20, no. 3/4 (2003): 107–130; W. L. White, M. Boyle, and D. Loveland, "Alcoholism/Addiction as a Chronic Disease: From Rhetoric to Clinical Reality" (2014), doi:10.4324/9781315821269.

6. M. Dennis, C. K. Scott, and R. Funk, "An Experimental Evaluation of Recovery Management Checkups (RMC) for People with Chronic Substance Use Disorders," *Evaluation and Program Planning* 26, no. 3 (2003): 339–352, doi:10.1016/S0149-7189(03)00037-5.

Chapter 10: Treatment Challenges and Solutions

1. T. R. Kosten and T. P. George, "The Neurobiology of Opioid Dependence: Implications for Treatment," *Science and Practice Perspectives* 1, no. 1 (2002): 13–20, doi:10.1151/spp021113.

2. T. R. Kosten and T. P. George, "The Neurobiology of Opioid Dependence: Implications for Treatment," *Science and Practice Perspectives* 1, no. 1 (2002): 13–20, doi:10.1151/spp021113.

3. National Institute on Drug Abuse, "Media Guide," October 2016, https://www.drugabuse.gov/publications/media-guide.

4. L. Selby, "Opioid Use Disorders: What Does Treatment Look Like?" *The DO,* May 27, 2016, http://thedo.osteopathic.org/2016/05/opioid-use-disorders-what-does-treatment-look-like.

5. Substance Abuse and Mental Health Services Administration (SAMHSA), "Adverse Childhood Experiences," last updated September 5, 2017, https://www.samhsa.gov/capt/practicing-effective-prevention/prevention-behavioral-health/adverse-childhood-experiences.

6. M. T. Merrick, K. A. Ports, D. C. Ford, T. O. Afifi, E. T. Gershoff, and A. Grogan-Kaylor, "Unpacking the Impact of Adverse Childhood Experiences on Adult Mental Health," *Child Abuse and Neglect* 69 (2017): 10–19, doi:10.1016/j.chiabu.2017.03.016.

7. M. Forster, A. L. Gower, I. W. Borowsky, and B. J. McMorris, "Associations Between Adverse Childhood Experiences, Student-Teacher Relationships, and Non-Medical Use of Prescription Medications Among Adolescents," *Addictive Behaviors* 68 (2017): 30–34, doi:10.1016/j.addbeh.2017.01.004.

8. K. M. Lawson, S. E. Back, K. J. Hartwell, M. Moran-Santa Maria, and K. T. Brady, "A Comparison of Trauma Profiles among Individuals with Prescription Opioid, Nicotine or Cocaine Dependence," *American Journal of Addiction* 22, no. 2 (2013): 127–131, doi:10.1111/j.1521-0391.2013.00319.x.

9. Substance Abuse and Mental Health Services Administration, National Center for Trauma-Informed Care and Alternatives to Seclusion and Restraint, "Trauma-Informed Approach and Trauma-Specific Interventions," last updated April 27, 2018, https://www.samhsa.gov/nctic/trauma-interventions.

10. Hazelden Betty Ford Foundation, "Frequently Asked Questions about Medication-Assisted Treatment for Opioid Addiction," http://www.hazeldenbettyford.org/treatment/models/mat-faq#thirteen.

11. Hazelden Betty Ford Foundation, Butler Center for Research, "Research Update: Prescription Opioids and Dependence," January 2016, https://www.hazelden.org/web/public/document/research-update-opioids.pdf.

12. National Council for Behavioral Health, "Identifying and Lifting Barriers to Integrating MAT with 12 Step Modalities," May 25, 2017, https://www.thenationalcouncil.org/wp-content/uploads/2017/06/MAT-with-12-Steps-slide-deck.pdf.

Appendix A

1. Johns Hopkins Medicine, "CAGE Substance Abuse Screening Tool," https://www.hopkinsmedicine.org/johns_hopkins_healthcare/downloads/CAGE%20Substance%20Screening%20Tool.pdf.

2. See National Institute on Drug Abuse, "Chart of Evidence-Based Screening Tools for Adults and Adolescents," page last updated February 2018, https://www.drugabuse.gov/nidamed-medical-health-professionals/tool-resources-your-practice/screening-assessment-drug-testing-resources/chart-evidence-based-screening-tools-adults.

3. SAMHSA-HRSA Center for Integrated Health Solutions, "Screening Tools," www.integration.samhsa.gov/clinical-practice/screening-tools#drugs.

4. S. D. Passik, K. L. Kirsh, and D. Casper, "Addiction-Related Assessment Tools and Pain Management: Instruments for Screening, Treatment Planning, and Monitoring Compliance," *Pain Medicine* 9 (2008): S145–S166, doi:10.1111/j.1526-4637.2008.00486.x.

5. D. A. Tompkins, G. E. Bigelow, J. A. Harrison, R. E. Johnson, P. J. Fudala, and E. C. Strain, "Concurrent Validation of the Clinical Opiate Withdrawal Scale (COWS) and Single-Item Indices

Duplicating this page is illegal. Do not duplicate without the publisher's written permission.

115

against the Clinical Institute Narcotic Assessment (CINA) Opioid Withdrawal Instrument," *Drug and Alcohol Dependence* 105, no. 1–2 (2009): 154–159, doi:10.1016/j.drugalcdep.2009.07.001.

6. T. Munder, F. Wilmers, R. Leonhart, H. W. Linster, and J. Barth, "Working Alliance Inventory-Short Revised (WAI-SR): Psychometric Properties in Outpatients and Inpatients," *Clinical Psychology and Psychotherapy* 17, no. 3 (2010): 231–239, doi:10.1002/cpp.658.

7. W. R. Miller and J. S. Tonigan, "Assessing Drinkers' Motivation for Change: The Stages of Change Readiness and Treatment Eagerness Scale (SOCRATES)," *Psychology of Addictive Behaviors* 10, no. 2 (1996): 81–89, doi:10.1037/0893-164X.10.2.81.

8. Center for Substance Abuse Treatment, *Enhancing Motivation for Change in Substance Abuse Treatment,* Treatment Improvement Protocol (TIP) Series, No. 35, HHS Publication No. (SMA) 13-4212 (Rockville, MD: Substance Abuse and Mental Health Services Administration, 1999), https://store.samhsa.gov/product/TIP-35-Enhancing-Motivation-for-Change-in-Substance -Abuse-Treatment/SMA13-4212.

9. Center for Substance Abuse Treatment, *Enhancing Motivation for Change in Substance Abuse Treatment,* Treatment Improvement Protocol (TIP) Series, No. 35, HHS Publication No. (SMA) 13-4212 (Rockville, MD: Substance Abuse and Mental Health Services Administration, 1999), https://store.samhsa.gov/product/TIP-35-Enhancing-Motivation-for-Change-in-Substance -Abuse-Treatment/SMA13-4212.

10. C. C. DiClemente, D. Schlundt, and L. Gemmell, "Readiness and Stages of Change in Addiction Treatment," *American Journal on Addictions* 13, no. 2 (2004): 103–119, doi:10 .1080/10550490490435777.

11. Center for Substance Abuse Treatment, *Enhancing Motivation for Change in Substance Abuse Treatment,* Treatment Improvement Protocol (TIP) Series, No. 35, HHS Publication No. (SMA) 13-4212 (Rockville, MD: Substance Abuse and Mental Health Services Administration, 1999), https://store.samhsa.gov/product/TIP-35-Enhancing-Motivation-for-Change-in-Substance-Abuse -Treatment/SMA13-4212.

Appendix C

1. Center for Substance Abuse Treatment, *Enhancing Motivation for Change in Substance Abuse Treatment,* Treatment Improvement Protocol (TIP) Series, No. 35, HHS Publication No. (SMA) 13-4212 (Rockville, MD: Substance Abuse and Mental Health Services Administration, 1999), https://store.samhsa.gov/product/TIP-35-Enhancing-Motivation-for-Change-in-Substance -Abuse-Treatment/SMA13-4212.

2. Center for Substance Abuse Treatment, *Detoxification and Substance Abuse Treatment,* Treatment Improvement Protocol (TIP) Series, No. 45, HHS Publication No. (SMA) 15-4131 (Rockville, MD: Center for Substance Abuse Treatment, 2006), https://store.samhsa.gov/product /TIP-45-Detoxification-and-Substance-Abuse-Treatment/SMA15-4131.

ABOUT HAZELDEN PUBLISHING

As part of the Hazelden Betty Ford Foundation, Hazelden Publishing offers both cutting-edge educational resources and inspirational books. Our print and digital works help guide individuals in treatment and recovery, and their loved ones. Professionals who work to prevent and treat addiction also turn to Hazelden Publishing for evidence-based curricula, digital content solutions, and videos for use in schools, treatment programs, correctional programs, and electronic health records systems. We also offer training for implementation of our curricula.

Through published and digital works, Hazelden Publishing extends the reach of healing and hope to individuals, families, and communities affected by addiction and related issues.

For more information about Hazelden publications, please call **800-328-9000** or visit us online at **hazelden.org/bookstore.**